MANAGE

MY EMOTIONS

What I Wish I'd Learned in School
About Anger, Fear, and Love

Kenneth J. Martz, Psy.D.

1st Printing Edition, 2020

ISBN: 978-1-7357109-1-4 (print)

ISBN: 978-1-7357109-0-7 (digital)

www.DrKenMartz.com

PRAISE FOR MANAGE MY EMOTIONS

Sound advice, and his passion for the subject matter clearly comes across.

**Huge Orange Publication Review,
Five Star Rating, Editor's Pick Winner**

Definitely helps readers to become masters of their emotions. There are many suggestions throughout the book on how we can manage our emotions...A highly recommended read for those who are looking for ways to manage their emotions better!

Tommy Wong for Readers' Favorite, Five Star Rating

Promises a clear and happy mind, and I highly recommend it to anyone who wishes to achieve it.

Rabia Tanveer for Readers' Favorite, Five Star Rating

Frankly, exactly the book I needed as I wade through the isolation and personal slump that a worldwide pandemic has forced on us... This is an easy book for me to recommend highly and I believe it will resonate with many other readers.

Jamie Michele for Readers' Favorite, Five Star Rating

Reflects well the head and heart of a competent, compassionate author. Manage your emotions and learn to live well! Read on.

**Dr. Sandra Rasmussen, Author of <u>Ready, Set, Go! Addiction
Management for People in Recovery</u>**

Kind, hopeful, and encouraging... Perfect for those seeking a new or deeper perspective on emotions

Book Review Directory

Filled with exercises to get at the root of unwanted feelings. I took notes for my own use as I was editing it! I know the advice, and especially the practical exercises, will help a lot of people.

Penny Fletcher, Author/Editor at Write Your Heart Out

Dr. Martz does an outstanding job of offering solutions to manage our emotions, and prevent them from sabotaging our life goals. His 25 years of experience in the fields of Mental Health and Addiction allows for insight and perspective that few can give.

Joel Elston, Author of <u>The Bench</u>

TABLE OF CONTENTS

To the Roses,
as well as the Thorns in my life

Thanks for your support
throughout this journey
toward balance.

Free Gifts!

Be sure to check out my website at www.DrKenMartz.com for updates on free material, seminars, forthcoming books, and more.

From there, you can download a range of free tools to support your journey, such as

- Emotion Circle
- How to Meditate
- Relaxation Techniques
- Manage My Emotions Checklist

Join Dr. Ken's Meditation School, our Facebook support group with others who are beginning meditation or other life practices. You can ask questions and share success!

https://drkensmeditationschool.thinkific.com/ to see the Beginner's Meditation Blueprint training with free preview guided meditation. For a limited time, use discount code SPRINGBREAKBOOK50 for 50% off.

INTRODUCTION

In deciding to write this book, I needed to consider several important questions. Why now? Why this topic? Why would anyone pick this up today? The answers came swiftly. As I write in this age of COVID-19, there is perhaps no more important time and topic. With the isolation and strife of today's environment, it is a time for healing, connecting, and rebuilding.

As a licensed psychologist, I was trained in the practice of limiting self-disclosure. My story is not as important as yours. In this case, however, I offer a piece of my story to help frame and understand the chapters you are about to read.

This book is the evolution of a story starting long ago. I remember as a child reading Henry David Thoreau and being engaged by his reflections on Walden Pond. He wrote, "I went to the woods because I wished to live deliberately, to put to rout all that was not life, and not when I come to die, discover that I had not lived." Over the years, I have supported efforts to maintain Walden Pond, and a picture of it hangs in my family room, quietly reminding me to consider what is truly important.

In my clinical work, I often speak of the importance of emotions. I remember a time when I was on a televised discussion of a psychology topic. Two days later, a client stopped me and said, "I saw you on TV on Tuesday." She smiled and jokingly continued, "You couldn't make it two minutes without talking about emotions." Setting her joking aside, I considered the deep truth in this, what if emotions are central to our "selves," our relationships, our success, and maybe even to filling that lingering hunger in our lifelong search for meaning?

Thoreau also said that the masses live lives of quiet desperation. I have always struggled against this quote. Perhaps you have as well. So much of our lives are spent in boring, benign maintenance, like washing dishes, folding laundry, shopping, and cleaning. For many, work outside the home takes effort, pays the bills, and perhaps even has meaning, but lacks day-to-day passion and enjoyment due to office politics and other strains.

So where is the time that is left after we do what we must, to live the passion of life? What do we do with this time? What if emotions and love were the center of it, rather than the goal of it? What if I could better understand emotions and the role they play in motivation? What if I could feel confident in having tools to manage the less comfortable emotions more effectively? What if I knew how to prevent my less comfortable emotions from causing damage to my relationships and to myself?

I went to school to learn about these issues. They taught lots of things about the brain and thinking, and disorders. I want to know more than illness, but rather what makes us well and what makes us thrive. Some of the most important solutions I have found along the way, deepening over time, experience, awareness, and practice.

I have spent a lifetime considering these questions. The answers are out there. Some of them are shared in the coming pages. I invite you to join me as we work through these issues and seek more in this ongoing journey together. We can do this. Together. Each step gets easier and stronger, just as we practice in life.

This book is developed so that the topics build upon each other. You may find yourself tempted to skip ahead to "the chapter" that discusses "your issue," or you may find yourself reading straight through since sometimes these other topics are related. Like an onion, each of the pieces are linked, and each chapter peels an interconnected layer. For this reason, I encourage you to read straight through, even if you think the topic does not apply to you. However, you approach this journey, let's get started.

In Part 1 of this book, we will examine some background information that is needed context for all the information that follows. In Part 2, we will consider the basic process of emotional change. In Part 3, we can begin to explore the impacts of specific emotions, as well as a range of tools for each. In Part 4, we review how our personal emotions interact in multiple external situations such as relationships and the workplace.

You can also feel free to check out my website, where you will find new resources and tools to support along this ongoing journey at www.DrKenMartz.com

Now begins this practice of emotions.

PART 1:

INTRODUCTION TO EMOTION

CHAPTER 1

WHERE AM I NOW?
\\\\\\\ /////

"Let's start at the very beginning,
a very good place to start..."
- Julie Andrews

It is best to start where we are today. There are no judgments about what we have not done in the past. We did the best we could with the tools we had learned. Perhaps that is why we are here together, to share and grow skills so that tomorrow can be different. What is it that drew you to this book? What is it you hope to learn? How important is that to you? These are important questions. You may be motivated but want a quick answer. So, go ahead and jump ahead to the topic that calls to you. It is OK. But then, come back here, start at the beginning, and continue. The topics in this book build on one another. So later chapters are easier to understand if you have completed the earlier chapters. So, be here now. Take a moment to answer some questions and take the time to practice the exercises along the way.

This is your journey, so enjoy it rather than rush it. There are flavors of ice cream that I had never tried. I was too busy and set in my ways, eating the same flavor (which I still love). Now though, I have tried many flavors. Some I did not like, but now there are many others that I love. This is why we are together:

- To learn more about the range of life through the language of emotions.

- To broaden our range of flavors of emotions rather than being stuck with one.

- To come to life more fully

Let's begin with some simple questions. There are no right or wrong answers. There are no trick questions, although some may be tricky, as you will understand later. I encourage you to take the time to think about these questions and to write down your answers. You may wish you had, later.

- Why did I pick up this book?

- What do I hope to learn?

- Am I satisfied with all the areas of my life?

- How would I like my life to be different?

- Am I worthy of such a change?

- Am I able to commit to the effort needed to achieve this goal?

- Am I willing to commit to the effort needed to achieve this goal?

- Starting when?

- Do I understand why I have these emotions?

- Which emotion is most troubling to me (there may be more than one)?

- What sensations occur in my body when I experience this feeling?

- What thoughts go through my head when I have this feeling?

- What images go through my mind when I have this feeling?
- Does it seem like this feeling is permanent?
- Is this feeling permanent?
    - If I think the answer is Yes, am I absolutely sure?
- What does this feeling need to be able to change?
- Am I willing to acknowledge my blind spots?
- Do I have the tools I need to make changes?
- Do I have a diverse toolbox of coping strategies?
- Do I know how my brain works, in basic terms?
- Do I know how my autopilot mind sets me up for trouble or happiness?
- Has trauma affected my emotions?
- Am I aware of the emotional baggage I carry from my past?
- Am I aware of a range of things that make me feel fear, anger, joy, compassion, and respect?
- Am I aware of how my emotions have impacted my relationships?
- Do I understand the role of emotional patterns in the development of addictive behavior patterns?
- Does my culture affect my experience of emotion?
- When I make changes, do I know how to effectively make them remain consistent?

You may notice that some of the answers to these questions are easy, and some are difficult. You may find that some are complicated. As we journey together through this book, you will be able to answer differently. Each chapter will have different exercises to explore and deepen your understanding of the topic, to practice the application of tools, and to learn new skills that will be used later. Take the time to complete the exercises. They build on one another, so later exercises may be less effective if you did not practice the earlier ones. Again, this is your journey. Approach it as you please. These are simply suggestions to help get the most from this process.

I must confess. I write these suggestions because I know that I also want to jump to the solutions in life. Over time, I have learned to understand that often the solution is not what I expected, so I would have skipped to the wrong chapter.

My current perspective can also change. When I resolve one surface issue, I have often found a new one underneath. Together, as we continue this journey, we get more of that feeling we are searching to find.

CHAPTER 2

THE ROLE OF EMOTION
❖❖❖❖❖❖ ❖❖❖❖❖

The best and most beautiful things in
the world cannot be seen or even touched
- they must be felt with the heart.
\- Helen Keller

Why Do We Have Emotion?

Our moods have developed over thousands of years. They have a wide range of benefits as well as pitfalls. By and large, consider that they are there to help us, and they have served us for many thousands of years. Unfortunately, they never came with a user's manual, which can leave us frustrated, embarrassed, and confused.

Benefits of Emotions

Happiness, love, passion, strength; there is a wide range of emotions that help us know when we are headed in the right direction. Animals know that sweet berries are safe to eat, and bitter berries are unsafe. Just the same, as we become aware of our emotions, we can use them to help guide us into greater effectiveness, deepen positive relationships, be more productive, and therefore feel more fulfilled. When my emotions consistently make me feel good, that helps to motivate me to continue.

Even the "negative" emotions are very valuable. They have precious lessons to teach us when we are off track. If I lie or cheat in life, fear, and anger often follow. Their discomfort helps to guide me back. "Negative" emotions also help us to appreciate the "positive" emotions even more. I do not want anyone to feel sadness, but once I experience it, my joys feel all the sharper in contrast. I love ice cream, but some days there is a bit of "rocky road." I may never taste all the flavors out there, but the more I know, the more I appreciate my favorite. (I'd say which one is my favorite, but it changes over time, with my mood and even my environment, but more on that later).

Challenges of Emotions

When we do not know how to manage our emotions, there can be a range of harms done to our work, our relationships, and ourselves. We can become "stuck" in an "unresolved" issue, or emotions can flare like an uncontrolled flame.

Being "stuck" leaves us unnecessarily reliving old wounds. It is like having a thorn stuck in your foot. It will continue to irritate and be painful; it may get worse at times and better at times. You may someday realize that it is worse when you are walking and stops hurting when you sit down, as you begin to manage the lingering pain. At worst, it can become infected, damaging your whole body. How much better would it have been if you had learned to pull out the thorn as soon as possible?

Emotions can also flare up uncontrollably. Sometimes we get angry and perhaps yell, or worse. Next, even after the anger calms, there were wounds that it caused because of our *uncontrolled expression,* on top of the issue that made us angry in the first place. Sometimes these thorns need to be removed as well.

The Challenge of Emotional Collections

One of the emotional challenges is that we tend to collect negative experiences and carry them around with us. This excess baggage can weigh us down, drain our energy, and leave us unable to manage life. Said another way, perhaps you collected an embarrassing moment with friends at age 8, got angry with a disappointment from mom at age 11, were scared of a public presentation in school at age 15, got dumped by the "love of your life" at age 17, were yelled at by your boss at age 24, and were in a terrifying car accident at age 30; struggled sleepless nights with your sick child at age 34, buried your parents at age 38, and on and on.

Are these simple memories, or do we linger with "unresolved" emotions from these times? Do we know how to lay down the baggage from the past and find freedom? If not, life becomes heavy, depressing and difficult, anxious and frustrating, or perhaps cold and lonely. When past hurts are not properly managed, they can become filters that harm us today, perhaps we are aware of it, and perhaps it is purely on our "autopilot."

Balance of Emotional Management

Emotions are often seen as a weakness, but when they are balanced, they can make the mother lion a fiercely loving companion. Emotions can be seen as negative, but they are only seen that way in relationship to their positive counterpart. The more I love my spouse, the more it hurts to be apart. Should I avoid all relationships to avoid the hurt of missing my beloved? We have successes in life in direct relationship to the risks we take. The same is true with emotions.

Emotional management is not the avoidance of emotions but rather the skill of balancing them so we can learn the lessons they teach, prevent unnecessary challenges, and shift emotions to a more pleasurable balance. Emotions run the risk of being painful, of becoming baggage, of hurting us and those around us rather than teaching us lessons so we can function better the next time. This is why this work is so important; to manage these risks and grow beyond.

What If I Don't Have A Range of Emotions?

Everyone has a wide range of emotions. Just as there is a constant flow of our inhalation and exhalation, our emotions ebb and flow. Sometimes they may be more intense, such as a flare of anger. Sometimes one or two may be more pronounced, such as weeks of grief after the death of a loved one. Sometimes we may even be unaware of the subtle changes.

How Do I Become Aware of Emotions?

Like many other areas in life, whatever we practice, we become better at it. There will be many practice examples throughout this book that work together to learn different lessons about emotions. Life is a natural laboratory teaching us these lessons, although, without a guide, the learning process can be slow and painful. By practicing emotional exercises throughout this book, we can build awareness and skill in navigating our internal emotional landscape.

The Body and Mind Connection

The body and mind are closely linked. When the body feels a certain empty sensation in the stomach, it tells the mind which says, "I'm hungry." Similarly, when the mind decides to go for a walk, it directs the body, which then stands up to begin walking. It is easy to see this link with behaviors, but the same is true for emotions. Let's explore this with a simple awareness exercise:

Awareness Exercise

Take a moment to find a comfortable seated posture. Close your eyes, and just let everything go. Choose a memory from a time when you felt a mild disappointment. How old were you; where were you located, and were you standing or sitting? What time of day was it? Think about this memory in detail. Were there any sounds in the room? Who else was present in the room? Whatever this moment was, take a moment to draw awareness inward, into the body, and notice what is happening in your body right now. Which muscles feel tight? Which muscles feel relaxed? Are there any changes that you notice in your breathing? Do you notice any changes in your belly or heart, or head?

Now imagine for a moment a time when you were annoyed; not an intense anger, but there was a disappointment that made you feel frustrated and distracted. Once again, scan your body to notice what is happening in your body right now. Are there any muscles that are tense or relaxing? Are there any muscles that are softening, or are there any muscles that are tight? Notice any changes in your belly, or in your heart, or in your shoulders, or in your face. What's happening in your hands and arms?

Letting this image go, call to mind a moment where you were successful with something. Recall the specific time and memory. Where were you? Were you standing or sitting? What time of day was it? Was there anyone else in the room? As you do this, notice what is happening in your body. What changes are happening in the shoulders, in the belly, in the heart, and in the jaw? Are any muscles becoming more tense? Notice what changes are happening. Are the muscles becoming more relaxed? Do you notice any changes in breathing? Changes in tension? Changes in body weight or pressure? Begin to step back from even this pleasurable memory and notice how quickly the body has changed and shifted. Notice how the body responded immediately to the memory that you noted. As you are ready, return to the room.

The body responds immediately to our thoughts, be they positive or negative. Notice also how each memory has a different response pattern of physical sensations in the body. Some emotions will be associated with certain sensations of heaviness or lightness, opening or closing, or other sensations across the body. These subtle changes often go unnoticed in our daily life. However, if we begin to bring our awareness to our emotional world, it may evolve as we develop greater awareness of the subtle changes of emotion and its effects on the body.

Awareness of Emotions is Healing

It's important to remember that awareness alone is healing. Notice how important it is to be aware. For example, when a baby is crying, sometimes it does not need to be fed. It does not need to be changed. It does not need anything other than for the parent to hold the child. Sometimes simply holding the child in awareness can ease the tension, and no other action is necessary. Oftentimes we rush off to find solutions when the simple solution of awareness and patience is exactly the right intervention. At times this may not be the proper intervention but consider which situations might benefit from awareness. Which situations might benefit from pausing a moment to gain a full understanding rather than reacting impulsively?

As we develop awareness over time, we can consider awareness of physical sensations, emotions, thoughts, and mental images. We can

14

also expand beyond ourselves to become aware of the interactions with our relationships, our culture, and the world.

Awareness Versus Autopilot

Over ninety percent of our lives are spent on autopilot. We typically don't spend much time thinking about breathing, digesting our food, and many other things we do. We are often unaware of activities we engage in, such as watching TV, passively consuming the present moment. Similarly, we may have many routines, such as our morning rituals, as we get ready to go to work. There are many times when we are sleepwalking through life, responding to it, rather than being aware and actively choosing directions.

In contrast, there are moments when we are actively aware and making decisions. For example, what am I going to have for dinner tonight? Once I make the decision, I mindlessly go about obtaining or preparing that meal. Another example can be seen in our work life. Do we actively choose our job, school, or other vocation each day, or do we largely go back again because it is what we did yesterday? Often decision points are brief moments of awareness in an otherwise continuously flowing life.

To a large extent, this works very well. The problem is that when we have an unhealthy pattern or habitual feeling state, we similarly continue on the same path. Perhaps we then label ourselves as "depressed" or "an anxious person," and then we continue the same pattern based on that conclusion. When driving, it is easy to continue the same path, but in the same way, it only takes a moment of awareness to wake up and change direction. These moments of awareness are critical to self-directed change, however fleeting.

When I began this journey years ago, like many men, I thought emotions were a distraction from the goal of the day. Through the years, I have learned more and more about the range of emotions and deepened my appreciation for them.

Developing awareness, this journey becomes more and more precious.

CHAPTER 3

COPING SKILLS/TRAINING
\\\\\\ //////

*Always be true to your feelings, because the more
you deny what you feel, the stronger it becomes.*
- Anonymous

*Never make permanent decisions
based on temporary feelings.*
- Anonymous

In the discussion of stress, we considered how protective factors and strengths might allow us to manage greater levels of stress and challenges. Most of us know this kind of management as coping skills. Coping skills are the strategies that we use to manage the challenges that face us. It is important to consider four areas regarding coping skills. How effective am I with a specific skill? What is my range of skills? How well is that skill matched to the specific problem area, and is there another skill that would be better, even though it is not in my skill set? So, let's examine each of these four areas.

What are Some of the Most Common Coping Skills?

Denial

Denial is a refusal to believe that a situation exists. The benefit of this coping style is that it allows us to function without needing to address the problem area. The risk of this coping style is that some problems go unaddressed may become worse. One example of this is substance use disorder, which may progress when untreated.

Repression/Numbing

Similar to denial, this involves putting the situation out of your conscious awareness. However, this is less intense than denial since a person can return to awareness by choice, or if someone were to ask a question about the situation that is being avoided.

Escape/Avoidance

Escape or avoidance is similar to denial in that it does not address the situation directly. However, avoidance includes an active movement away from the situation. A limitation of this strategy is that it keeps a person actively engaged with the problem area without offering any resolution to the problem. A benefit of this strategy is that it moves the person to a safer position. If there was a fire in the house, and I used denial as a coping skill, the fire would grow, and I would be in grave danger by using avoidance. I would be safer because I am actively running out of the house, however, some fires could have been contained quickly if they were addressed early rather than allowed to progress until they fell into the categories of denial or avoidance.

Rumination

Rumination is the active engagement of the problem area. When doing this, a person is often considering many angles and aspects about the impact of potential resolutions. The limitation of this strategy is that it can cause an uncomfortable paralysis as one continues to experience concern over the problem area. The benefit of this approach is that it focuses attention on solutions even though none is specifically chosen.

Rationalization

Rationalization is the use of my mind to separate myself from the emotions associated with the situation. The benefit of this coping strategy is that it allows decision-making objectivity based on predetermined values. The limitation is that this coping strategy limits our ability to connect emotionally with those involved in the situation with us. An example of this would be a business executive who makes difficult decisions for an organization even if that decision is not the same one that they would want for their own family member.

Applying Coping Strategies

While there are several coping strategies, it may be that I'm best with one or another. Considering the strengths and weaknesses of my preferred coping strategy, I can know the most effective use of it, as well as be aware of the limitations that I may face in handling situations.

Flexibility

Some individuals use one (and only one) coping strategy. I can be very effective working with a hammer, however in life, sometimes a wrench is better. Different tools are needed depending upon what the solution requires, so having more tools in my coping skill toolbox can increase my chances of success.

Tool Management

In addition to having a range of tools, it is important to know which tool is best for a given situation. For example, there are some situations where denial may be the best approach; there may be some situations where avoidance is the best approach; and it may be that in some situation's rumination is the best approach. Having skill not only in your range of tools but also in when and how to change tools when needed is very important.

Coping skills training is the process of learning about a range of tools identifying my existing patterns; identifying what areas I can grow in, and practicing the use of alternative coping strategies, so I become skilled in a range of approaches for whatever is needed. Sometimes a direct approach is best, and sometimes, an indirect approach may be more beneficial. Sometimes no intervention is useful, and sometimes pausing to wait for additional opportunities to arise may be beneficial. Coping skills training helps develop the wisdom to know what is needed, rather than simply reacting based on the tool that happens to be in my hand at the time.

Self-Assessment of Coping

Do a self-assessment review of each of the coping strategies we've discussed and mark which ones you have used in the last month. Identify which are the top two coping strategies you commonly use. Identify a recent stressful situation in your life based on your list of coping strategies. What has been your attempt to resolve that stressor? Consider if you have been rigid in your approach, only using one strategy. Consider the level of thoughtfulness that went into choosing that strategy as compared to other strategies.

Consider whether another one of these strategies might have been better than the one approach that you have chosen. You can repeat this exercise regarding several stressful situations to deepen your understanding of your habitual approaches, and then you will begin to understand how and why you choose those particular strategies.

Contextual Abilities

Sometimes, different situations call for different strategies. For example, someone may use different approaches in the workplace, as compared to working with their children, or as compared to approaches they use with their friends. Note that we may be comfortable with some strategies in one environment but not in another environment. Consider alcohol, for example. When I'm stressed, alcohol is an effective tool to quickly reduce tensions in the body. This may be effective in a single event. However, this may not be effective if it is the only tool that I use to manage every stressor. If I use this tool all the time, it may lead to alcoholism; or, at the least, excessive use of alcohol. This may not be an appropriate tool when I am stressed on the worksite. This may not be an effective tool for use when spending time with my children. This may not be an effective tool if I do not have a range of other coping approaches to use as needed.

Application of Coping Strategies

Let's consider some examples of how coping strategies work, particularly around denial and repression.

Denial: I Don't Do That

Denial sounds so horrible. Obviously, I would never do that. Unfortunately, it is the coping mechanism that "only" other people can do, by definition.

Consider: Can you think of three things you are in denial about? OK, how about 1? If I am in denial, I wouldn't know... So, of course, the answer to this is... No, I can't think of any. This makes denial a particularly challenging issue. It also becomes most problematic since what I cannot see; I cannot change.

So how do I become aware of something I am in denial about? It starts by asking this very question. The first step is to realize that there may be things I am unaware of. Then start to look for them. Examples to consider:

- I have this growth on my hand, but it's nothing serious.

- I have this pain in my chest, but I can handle it and keep running another mile.

- I'm a good driver. I won't get in an accident if I put on some makeup while driving.

- I am a good driver. I won't get in an accident if I go five miles over the speed limit.

- I live in a safe neighborhood. No one would ever go in my car.

- I have plenty of money. It's no problem to buy this $8 cup of coffee/soda/water.

- That coworker hates me. He would never help me with this project.

Often, we carry blind spots that we can quickly overcome with a brief moment of openness and awareness. If you find yourself wondering why one of these examples was on the list, be open and aware, just a moment longer...

If I am in denial, I cannot change. So, ask yourself:

- *Am I willing to admit that I might be unaware of some personal flaws?*

- *Am I willing to have the courage to examine these emotions and patterns?*

Denial Versus the "Truth"

What if I am simply denying something that is not true? If I say the sky is red, and you say no, it's blue, that is simply a statement of fact....unless it is a sunrise, or I am color-blind, or I have red sunglasses on, or any number of special circumstances. We all know about aliens, and who shot JFK, and how the Earth was created, and we are very certain that the other opinion is simply wrong. There are many things that we will simply dismiss as false, which are indeed untrue...and sometimes there are things we dismiss that are true.

I remember when I was in grade school, there was a presidential election. I remember the kids in school taking sides and arguing about how my candidate is the best, and yours is "stupid", and you are "stupid" for believing in him. Kids who didn't know much more than the name of the candidate were full of such strong opinions, sure of who was right and who was wrong, fighting over it. Of course, on any given day, about half of us were wrong.

We have learned so much since then. Today, we can rise above our denial to maturely listen to opposing views and find ways that different perspectives may have some truth, and we are stronger for knowing how even the adversarial system of justice helps us. Well, this may be a lifelong process, especially if we remain in denial.

There are indeed some things that society agrees are "truths." Anyone who disagrees is labeled with a psychological disorder with fancy names for disagreeing with what is commonly believed, such as psychosis or dementia. Of course, there was a time when people thought that you would fall off the Earth if you went past the edge, or that the Earth was the center of the universe, and other things that later were proven untrue.

There are many excellent books on truth and the nature of reality. For this chapter, simply be aware that:

1) There are many things we are in denial of,
2) In most cases, that is OK, and
3) There are some things that we deny, which we could benefit from reconsidering.

Denial versus Repression:

Repression is a fancy term for a gentle denial that we can easily become aware of. While denial can be more challenging to break through, repression moves something out of awareness but is more temporary. For example, right now, many animals are being mistreated, children are going to bed hungry, and people are dying of violence. I am not paying any attention to these things, nor have I done so for the last hour. I push these images out of my mind since they are uncomfortable, but I can quickly know the truth of these situations and acknowledge them. For example, even though we deny the magnitude of risks, we know that distracted driving has *some* risk involved, and we can quickly change course and choose to wait to shave or put on makeup until later. For this reason, repression is much easier to change.

In contrast with the attitude that denial is bad, it is easy to see why we are all in denial/repression of many things at a given moment. There is simply so much suffering in the world. If we didn't block some of it out, we could be completely immobilized. This is a useful and powerful tool when used responsibly.

Denial and Projection

Consider how denial may work in combination with other dynamics. When I "project" anger onto someone else. I simultaneously deny it in myself. So how do we know where to look to find these types of emotions? Consider the following exercise:

> *Choosing someone I am angry with, what are three labels I have for them? Perhaps they are lazy, or insensitive, rude, unforgiving, or many other things.*
>
> *Now consider for a few moments how I act the same way.*

When we judge others, there is often an element in ourselves that does the same thing. As we become aware of the ways we are mean, lazy, or unforgiving, we move these issues out of denial and into awareness, where we can begin to make changes.

I used to think that everyone else was wrong and read all those books about how to fix "them." I would be happy as soon as my coworker, spouse, or friend would see how wrong they were. As I continued through this journey, it became increasingly clear how these defenses kept me from knowing myself. Once I understood this, I also found out that it is easier to change the one person I can, myself. Over time I learned more games these tricky emotions played.

CHAPTER 4

GAMES EMOTIONS PLAY

*Somewhere between love and hate lies confusion,
misunderstanding and desperate hope.*
- Shannon L. Alder

*Fear is a manipulative emotion that
can trick us into living a boring life.*
- Donald Miller

Emotions can be tricky. They play frustrating games to protect themselves. They can hide from the light of awareness, knowing that their darkness pales before the light. For this reason, it is important not only to be aware of the emotions themselves but also some of the elusive games they play. Consider this a game, that we can improve at, master over time, and perhaps have some fun along the way. These games are similar to coping strategies, but a little different, since they are more like a patterned strategy than a response to a single emotion.

The Games We Play

Hide and Seek

Just as children play by hiding behind a larger object, emotions can be hidden by distractions. Often the symptom we see is only the tip of the iceberg, so we need to look deeper.

Anger is a common example of this issue that can be easy to understand. Consider the person who recently lost their job and becomes very angry. They blame the boss. They blame the economy. They blame their coworker. Perhaps they yell and throw things. Perhaps they hire a lawyer. The anger is real, but what else may be hiding underneath? When working with anger, we must honor the anger. However, understand that anger is a mask for other emotions that hide beneath and know that at some point, those emotions must be addressed. If I do not pull out a weed by its root, it will grow again.

Fear very often hides beneath anger. Fear can feel weak, so I hide it in a stronger feeling like anger. Fear is a primal emotion, activating the fight/flight response, in this case, anger. Perhaps it is fear of having to tell my friends that I failed. Perhaps it is fear of losing money, impacting food, and shelter.

Guilt can often hide behind fear. Perhaps it is fear of facing my guilt and shame. Perhaps the fear is about facing my failure, shortcoming, or perceived inadequacy. Perhaps these are beliefs that I am "not good enough." Perhaps this reflects a wound from long ago, a vulnerability and secret shame, long unspoken. This is the work of therapy, understanding how current situations have deep roots. If you can address the roots, the tree will fall.

Sometimes psychotherapy can be mocked with parodies of the counselor parroting the words of the patient. For example:

- Patient: I am so angry at my boss!
- Therapist: So, I hear you saying you are so angry at your boss.
- Patient: That's what I said!

However, the therapy process is a little different. By listening closely to the experienced emotion, the counselor can move the experience deeper. The experience begins to reflect the underlying emotion and give words to it. For example:

- Patient: I am so angry at my boss!
- Therapist: So, I hear you saying you are so angry at your boss.
- Patient: Yeah! He yelled at me about not turning in my report again!
- Therapist: That is so frustrating, to be unable to stop his repeated attacks.
- Patient: Yeah, I tried so hard, but it's nerve-wracking to be unable to keep up with the workload.
- Therapist: You are so strong and conscientious; it is hard to be yelled at for making a mistake.
- Patient: Right. It is just like my dad. I could never get it right for him either.

It is important to understand that the presenting problem is real, but often incomplete. From inside the situation, I may not be able to see it differently, so shifting perspective can help.

"Not it."

Sometimes emotions hide from us. Remember the defense of denial. I may say or believe:

- I am not angry
- I am not scared
- I am not insensitive

These beliefs may go so deep that they are hidden in our blind spots. We may have a vague awareness but be too frightened or ashamed to admit these emotions. As we have discussed throughout this book, we have all of the emotions, to a greater or lesser degree. So, to resolve denial, it is important to look at the fear/shame that hides it. Also, we can begin to practice awareness of the ways we engage in that denied emotion.

Thich Nhat Hahn wrote a moving essay and poem, "Please call me by my true names." He considers how we are all connected, and so there are times in life when I play the "victim" and the "pirate," either directly or indirectly. As we become aware of these shadow emotions, we can become free of them.

For example, you may be afraid to admit to being insensitive because of an identity as a caring person. Yet, there may be many things you have done that could be seen as insensitive. Have you ever turned off the commercial for abandoned puppies, or wounded warriors, or cancer patients, or a children's hospital? While you may care about every one of these causes, we choose to focus on one(s) that we decided as priorities in our lives. Every one we choose to support is choosing not to support another.

To explore: Choose an emotion to work on. List three ways it is uncomfortable to admit that emotion. Then search for ways that this has been expressed in your life.

I Know You Are but What Am I?

Sometimes people use a defense called projection. It is uncomfortable to admit something in ourselves, so we claim that the other person is the cause. When I yell at you, you yell back at me. Then I blame you for being angry, rather than seeing how I contributed to this dance. While it may be exactly true that the other person is angry, hiding beneath that awareness may be our own emotions.

Another way to understand this is the concept of mental filters. When I wear rosy sunglasses, I see compassion everywhere I look. When I wear black sunglasses, I see sadness everywhere I look. When I wear red punishing sunglasses, I see punishment everywhere I look. Sometimes my filters cause the perception of emotions in others, even if they do not exist in others. It is my own misinterpretation that is the root, my own wound that causes the issue to be blamed on the other.

It's Not You. It's Me

No. You are not angry. I am bad.

This is the reverse of the prior game. Instead of blaming you, I blame myself. However, this is still a mask of the central issue. Consider, for example, the person who starts crying, not out of sadness, but out of fear of the other's anger. Sometimes my emotions are involved in a dance with others, creating a secondary gain that is not related to the original issue. As another example, sometimes someone who is expressively anxious causes others to

30

step in as caretakers. So, there are several ways that I can engage in an emotion not because I am experiencing that feeling but due to the larger learned gain of that behavior pattern.

The Blame Game

Sometimes we blame others and fail to take responsibility. I get angry at you for something you did. You respond by being angry at me for something I did. Suddenly we are screaming at one another for each other's faults. This battle can quickly turn into a fight over the words that were just said, so that the original concern gets lost and unaddressed.

In the movie Beauty and the Beast, there is an iconic moment where they are arguing:

> Belle: [Tending wound]
>
> Beast: That hurts!
>
> Belle: Well, if you hold still, it wouldn't hurt as much!
>
> Beast: If you hadn't run away, this wouldn't have happened!
>
> Belle: If you hadn't frightened me, I wouldn't have run away!
>
> Beast: Well, you shouldn't have been in the West Wing!
>
> Belle: Well, you should learn to control your temper.
>
> Belle: Now hold still. This may sting a little [Tends wound]. By the way, thank you for saving my life.
>
> Beast: You're welcome.

Notice how the fight quickly escalates to a blame game and loses sight of the original wound. Consider how there are other emotions still hiding underneath that were not addressed. Notice also how this fight was resolved. Either party can recognize the blame game and step away from it. Letting go and offering compassion and the simple respect of a "thank you" or "I'm sorry" can shift the tone and direction of the conversation.

> *To explore: Think of a fight that you have had with someone. Observe the blame game as it played out. Identify your personal role in the situation. Identify an "offramp" when you could have stopped blaming and instead apologized or done something else, ending the game.*

Keeping Score

A variation of the blame game is keeping score. However, it may be an internal rather than an external fight. For example, consider the situation at work where I ask a coworker to help with some tasks. They may become angry since I am so lazy, and they do so much for me, never getting anything in return (keeping score). Meanwhile, I am angry at them since I have so many additional duties. They should be offering to help me more often (keeping score).

Keeping score is a losing game. In any relationship, someone will always give more in one area and take more in another. I will always get in relation to what I give, although the exchange may not be immediately visible. For example, I may give to my children on a daily basis. I give food, clothes, toys, playtime, and love. While this may seem naturally imbalanced, are there things I get in return? Yes. For example, I get the satisfaction of fulfilling my duties, pleasure at seeing my family smile, and moments of gratitude when they say, "Thanks" or "I love you." These may be priceless.

> *To explore: Consider a relationship where I keep score. Make a list of all the things they give to me. Consider how to practice letting go of*

the baggage of days or years of them "owing me." Notice that some of this work is clearing my personal scorecard and baggage.

Karma Replay

Like keeping score, we may internally collect evidence of a problem. Sometimes a scenario replays repeatedly over time, in our relationships, as well as those around us. This can accumulate over time and be reinforced through our beliefs, emotions, and relationships over the course of years. Now, when I meet a new person, I expect that behavior of them as well, even if they have never— or would never— do such a thing. For example, we meet them expecting to be hurt, betrayed, judged, or abandoned. That is a lot to put on someone when you first meet. This creates a barrier to be overcome to get to a level playing field with this new (or existing) relationship.

> *To explore: What are some of the expectations you hold in relationships? Have these expectations been held for a long time? In what ways do they prevent you from meeting the person where they are? Are you willing to let go of your past baggage to be able to start a new future?*

Along this journey, sometimes I was tricked into thinking that the problem was right in front of me. However, sometimes I was only bothered by today's event because it triggered a replay of one of my past wounds. Once I remembered my old bruises, it was easier to manage my present-day coworker challenge.

CHAPTER 5

FEELINGS, EMOTIONS, AND FACTS
➤➤➤➤➤➤ ➤➤➤➤➤

If you are carrying strong feelings about something
that happened in your past, they may hinder
your ability to live in the present.
- Les Brown

In order to move on, you must understand why
you felt what you did and why you no longer need to feel it.
- Mitch Albom

I feel like I'm waiting for something
that isn't going to happen.
- Anonymous

Introduction to Labels and Filters

Emotions have become ingrained in our language. However, they have developed in our language in a way that makes it seem like a permanent identity. In the mental health world, there was a time when it was common to refer to individuals as their diagnosis. "My anxious patient," "The addict," "The depressed patient," are some examples. Aside from being stigmatizing, this conveys that the mood state is prominent and stable, perhaps more so than it is in reality. Once these labels become internalized, they become rigid filters of myself. Said another way, once I believe my label, I start to use it as the explanation of all my behaviors, for example:

- I didn't go out tonight because I'm depressed

- I went out tonight to escape my depression.

- I didn't go to the party because I was too anxious

- I went to the party because I was too worried about what they would think of me if I didn't go.

These filters then make it harder to escape this false belief of permanence. While there may be situations where a sensation is more lasting, typically, if I expect it will stay the same, I will not be looking for any changes as they occur. Note that this awareness of change is critical to growth, as discussed earlier.

Understood together, labels of emotions can be perceived as facts when they are merely perceptions. Consider the following: When I go to an amusement park and get on a roller coaster, the ride takes me slowly higher and higher. The anticipation and growing height cause my heart to race. I begin to sweat, and my palms become clammy. As the car tops over the crest of the hill, it picks up speed as we begin to fall, and I scream. Which emotion did I just have? Some might label this as terror. Others might label these sensations as excitement and joy. The sensations of this scenario are nearly identical. Yet the label we choose for that sensation and the meaning we give to that label can change our reactions and future behavior dramatically. Words matter. As these sensations become labeled as emotions, they become perceived as facts. What if emotions are not facts?

Perhaps sensations are facts, but once we label them, we add filters, associations, and meaning. Facts are objective, like 2+2=4. Emotions are subjective in many ways. While we may try to measure emotions, at best, we can estimate them. There are tools, for example, to "measure" depression. In reality, they measure many other ancillary issues such as "I have trouble falling asleep," I have lost my appetite," or perhaps, "I feel sad." These issues are not really measuring my internal experience of "sadness." As we begin to understand that emotions are not facts, we can be released from their control.

Respect for Emotions

This discussion is not in any way meant to imply that other's emotions are unimportant or should be judged. In fact, the reverse is true. When someone else is having an emotion, it is even more important to listen to the reality of their *perception* of their feeling state. Understanding their experience is critical in helping them soften and move beyond it. If you judge them, telling them that their feeling is not real, they may hold tighter to that interpretation and remain in that state. Listening to one's experience as they feel it is an important step in helping that person to be able to change. Wherever I want them to get to, it starts here, before helping them see the steps that lead out of that experience. Consider how you deeply understand this later, after many examples written in the following chapters that can help you understand the impermanence of emotions.

Emotions Deserve Respect

I respect my own emotions. I respect the emotions of others.

Wherever I am today, it is without judgment. I have come as far as I was able to, for today. As I learn new things today, this opens new possibilities for tomorrow. Sometimes people will get caught up in judging that they "should" have known, or learned, faster. This simply is not possible. There is the story of the young boy who had purchased caterpillars. In days, the caterpillars had built cocoons, and as days went by, the boy could see some wriggling of the cocoons and even some small holes in the cocoons. Anxious to help them, he ripped open the cocoons. All the butterflies died. Heartbroken, he turned to his father, crying. Dad gently explained that as the baby butterflies are in the cocoon, they press against the walls of their cages, growing stronger and stronger until they are able to break free. Without having built this strength, they are not able to fly.

We cannot rush success or change the evolution of our emotions. Just as children mature over the years, we learn more and more as time goes on. So, do not be limited by what you felt yesterday. The cocoon may be about to burst open today.

Perception and Misperception Exercise

Imagine for a moment you wake up early in the day, and you gradually go outside and suddenly see a snake. Immediately your body responds in one manner or another. Perhaps you run away quickly. Perhaps you grab a rake and attack the snake.

After attacking the snake or running away, we have a moment to pause, breathe, and regain our awareness. In doing so, perhaps we realize that what we thought was a snake was actually our garden hose. We misunderstood what it was in the early morning light.

Misperception is a common cause of intensive emotion. Taking a moment for reflective thought, rather than immediate reactiveness, can often prevent damaging responses. Most situations we face are not life-threatening, requiring immediate knee-jerk reactions. Instead, they are typically situations that could benefit from a moment of reflection to choose the most effective action.

Over the years, I have learned that some of my perceived "facts" were wrong. Then I learned I might care less about being "right" and more about being "happy." This perceptual shift can begin our journey inside, in the brain that processes these beliefs through filters and habits.

CHAPTER 6

EMOTIONS AND THE BRAIN
❙❙❙❙❙ ╱╱╱╱╱

Contentment and happiness depend solely on the mind,
not on external objects or circumstances.
- Amma

Our mind controls much of what we see and do, but there is no easy user's manual as it relates to emotions. Let's consider a few simple principles of how we learn and how behaviors become patterns which move into our unconscious.

Mirror Neurons

Mirror neurons are interesting cells in the brain that connect us and our emotions to the outside world. They are important for learning and related to social interactions in many ways. One example is when a baby chimpanzee sees his mother opening a nut. He watches how it is done and is then able to do it himself. We think of this as social learning, but mirror neurons in the brain help us to reflect internally regarding things that are seen externally. Another example is when we see certain facial expressions. These neurons activate similarly within ourselves. For example, when I see someone smile, I may spontaneously begin to smile myself. When I see someone frown, there may be a different reaction. That occurs immediately within my body. Think about this for a moment. When I see you smiling, these cells respond and react, reflecting that mood.

It's important to understand how social interactions are deeply ingrained into our brain physiology, and ultimately our health. A particular benefit to knowing this is that it assists us in learning from other people's successes and mistakes, so we do not need to make those mistakes ourselves. Another benefit is to realize how smiling at someone maybe one of the fastest and infectious ways to spread a positive mood and connection. As the saying goes, when you're smiling, the whole world smiles with you.

Sometimes this mirroring is spontaneous. There is also research that if I posture and move in a similar manner to you (mirroring you), this also resonates. It can increase feelings of congruence, agreeability, or disagreeability— and between us.

Learning

Three are two key methods of learning. One involves the repetition of routine facts. The other involves the storage of memory of intense emotion, even if it is a single event. Remember that learning includes not only the mental fact but also many aspects of the experience from the senses.

Rote Learning

A common form of learning is simple rote learning through repetition. This can be simple to understand.

Imagine for a moment that inside your brain, one cell is linked to the next cell, which links to the next cell, which links to the next cell, communicating information down a chain of connected cells. Imagine for a moment that you wanted to learn something like how to solve a kind of math problem. One of the most common ways to do this is through repetition. Just as we did in school, we may repeat our times tables mentally stating: five times five equals 25, five times five equals 25, five times five equals 25, five times five equals 25. This repetition, over time creates an ingrained memory. Just like repeated weightlifting at the gym, this repetition builds strength in the connections of this memory. This is one of the most common approaches to learning new material. The repetition strengthens our learning for a lifetime. This simple repetition can be strengthened by involving multiple parts of the brain. For example, instead of reciting my times tables if I write my times tables while saying them out loud, I will be engaging: 1) the kinesthetic part of my brain, which writes the words 2) the visual part of my brain, which sees the writing and 3) the auditory part of my brain which hears the repetition. Engaging additional parts of the brain assists learning.

Rote Learning and Emotions

In terms of emotions, this type of learning occurs naturally. As we have discussed, with each emotion, there will be physical sensations throughout the body. There will be sights and sounds and smells encoded in these memories. If the emotions are intense, this learning may occur even more quickly. Again, learning is beneficial. This learning makes it easier to be productive rather than being forced to repeat similar concerns again and again throughout time. However, when we learn lessons that are damaging, inaccurate, or debilitating, these can be difficult to unlearn. For example, if I was repeatedly embarrassed at home, there may be a range of emotions that occur. The associated fear, anger, and shame may hide through these neurological connections to the sights, sounds, and smells at the place of the repeated events. Knowing this can help us to understand how these uncomfortable memories may be retriggered when we accidentally encounter similar sights, sounds, or smells in the future. Once this memory is reactivated, it can trigger the emotions that are associated with it as well. It is as if we are reliving the moment of the past in this present moment.

As an example, consider Joey, who grew up in a two-bedroom apartment on the ground floor. On nights when his father would drink, he would become angry if his dinner was late or the house was not clean, becoming enraged and physically abusive. On one occasion, when he arrived home, the smell of alcohol was strong. His mother quickly sent him to his room to finish his homework. Moments later, Joey could hear shouting, crying, the smashing of dishes, and the sounds of skin hitting skin. Fast forward twenty years, and Joey is a person struggling with recovery from his alcohol use, trying to learn about his triggers. In this brief scenario, how many sights, sounds, feelings, emotions, thoughts, or other associations can you identify? Each one of these elements, from broken glass to relationships with older women, can activate these old memories and habitual patterns of how to manage safety. Similarly, we all have habitual ways we learned to deal with our fear, guilt, and anger. These patterns become habitual and tend to continue unless something changes.

Traumatic Learning/Flashbulb Memory

While our body learns effectively through repetition, sometimes experiences are painful or dangerous. These types of experiences are also stored in the brain but are done so quickly. For example, if I touch a hot stove, I learn very quickly about the pain and do not need to repeat the experience. This phenomenon is also called flashbulb memory. Years ago, when cameras had flashbulbs, someone would take our picture, and our eyes would be momentarily blinded by the flash with a colored after-image as the visual flash was "burned into" us. Flashbulbs and hot stoves are relatively harmless, but many of us experience intense acute traumas over the course of our lives, from car accidents, war, assaults, or other intense experiences. Consider also that this is not only for negative memories, causing avoidance, but also for positive experiences. So, if my first-time gambling or using drugs is experienced as a "big win" or euphoric experience, it can cause me to seek that pleasure again. This can be dangerous, developing an addictive pattern, or it can be healthy, bonding us with a loved one, such as the birth of a first child.

Permanence of Learning

Once we have learned something, how can we forget it? Once we have been burned or repeated something for days and years, is it possible to forget it? If I asked you to please forget what five times five equals, how would you do that? As you consider this, you may realize that there is not an easy way to do it. The only way that I have identified, which could disrupt such a memory, involved brain trauma such as traumatic brain injury or other severe degeneration like Alzheimer's disease. If we have learned certain lessons and cannot unlearn them, what can we do about it?

There may be two ways to approach this learning challenge: through rebuilding and re-framing.

Rebuilding

While I may not be able to change a memory, I may be able to create new memories that are different. For example, while I do not forget that a pot is hot, after days and years of effectively cooking, I can build trust in my ability to use that pot without being burned. Similarly, after a difficult ending of a romantic relationship, I can start a new relationship, building new experiences in a new context that contrasts the prior pain. In doing this, I can build a new trust in relationships in a more complex manner. So, my mental filters no longer simply say relationships are painful, but relationships are painful in certain general conditions (e.g., with that person) or certain precise conditions (or even with that person while using the behaviors and decisions that we chose then, but relationships are pleasurable in this new situation with the same person using the different types of behavior I have learned since).

Reframing

Reframing is another way to manage prior learning. For example, if the first person I ever ask out on a date laughs at me, the emotional response of embarrassment leads me to be afraid to ask others out on a date. I cannot change the past, so I can never change that event. I cannot change what I heard at that time. I cannot change the sights and sounds or behaviors or words of the past event. However, I can change my *present* interpretation of that event. For example, instead of interpreting that event as evidence that I should never date again, I could reinterpret the story with other meanings. For example, I could interpret it as a reflection that the other person was not ready for this relationship even though the request came from a good place in me. I could also reinterpret the situation, understanding that meeting the right person often requires repeated dates, just like in business, sometimes you need to make mistakes several times before being successful. It can be perceived that this particular rejection was one step closer to my goal of meeting and establishing a deeply loving and fulfilling relationship.

It's like climbing a set of stairs. I could take one step and complain that it was "too difficult" and "it's too far," or I can climb one step and see that I am closer to the goal with each step along the way. It doesn't change the distance, but mentally reframing the story can change the meaning and intensity of the feelings, which can bring more freedom from past events. In the case of childhood trauma, this can also be effective, reframing specific beliefs like "I was bad," or "It was my fault," to a broader understanding that "I was only eight years old; it was the adult's responsibility to maintain safety."

Autopilot

When we have simple or complex repeated behaviors, they often move into an unconscious autopilot. Understanding the brain, it is easy to see how it is designed to scan the environment, access thousands of elements of memories, and replay habitual shortcuts of how to respond to those situations. We are designed for an autopilot to automatically engage what we have learned as the best course of action. Said another way, wherever I am today, my best thinking got me here. If I want to do more, I need to learn more, to grow beyond my past. Similarly, the boss is not simply being a mean person, but rather following what he or she has learned as the most effective approach, not knowing another way. Put simply, if I knew a more effective approach, wouldn't I have done it? This is a core element in this book. No one is perfect. Everyone can improve, in many ways. Perhaps the first step is awareness of the need for change and a commitment to continued efforts. Just like a plant, if we are not growing, we are dying. It is an ongoing process of evolution.

Autopilot becomes an effective way to conserve mental energy as we perform routine, repetitive tasks such as folding laundry, washing dishes, driving, and other things we do mechanically. The risk comes in when unhealthy behaviors or moods move into autopilot. What starts to happen when I hate my boss for years on end? What starts to happen when I drink multiple drinks nightly for years on end? Strictly speaking, we are in control, but as the behavioral patterns are practiced, it becomes more and more difficult to realize their impact. We may even forget why we were angry at our boss or why we started drinking in the first place.

Mental Directories

Just like a computer, our brains have three major functions for memory: data input, memory storage, and data retrieval. First, we receive new information through our senses. For example, we may see an apple. Next, this information goes to our storage data banks, and the brain searches through the directory's in our brain for the sights, sound, smell, and taste of an apple, as well as every other time I've had the experience of "apple." This memory is then added to that file of all the other associations of apples in my data bank. Later there may be a time when I am asked an opinion of apples, and my mind can go to this directory to retrieve this list of memories regarding apples and find that the new one has been added.

Consider how this works with an emotion. I experience a moment of sadness and the memory of this present moment goes to the directory of all my other memories of sadness. Over time, the more I experienced memories of sadness, the fuller this directory will become. Now, if I ask you if it is a happy or sad world, your mind goes to this directory to compare it to the happy directory. We begin to experience all the compiled evidence of sadness as compared to all of our compiled evidence of happiness. This can become a filter for new experiences. When I expect the world to be sad, I begin to place new memories into that category, whether or not they belong there.

Mental Filters

Expectations become filters in the mind. Once I have decided that my boss is mean and insensitive, all new experiences that are recorded about him (or her) are filtered through this expectation. So, the next time my boss is late, it is perceived through the filter of insensitivity rather than a filter of compassion for what might have caused a legitimate delay. These filters are like wearing sunglasses. If I am wearing black sunglasses of depression, everywhere I look, I will see triggers of sadness. These triggers of sadness will be stored in my directory of sadness memories, and these memories will become evidence that I should be sad. However, if I wear rosy "denial" sunglasses, everywhere I look, there will be Pollyanna rainbows and unicorns. These will then be stored in my Pollyanna directory.

Understand the goal is not to throw away our sunglasses but to be aware of when we're wearing them and how they work, so we can:

- See reality
- Be able to select the proper memories and evidence
- Live with a little more ease, without the prejudgments caused by filters.

Once we wear sunglasses, for a while, it is easy to forget we are wearing them. Then there is the danger that we forget we're wearing them and the prejudices they cause. Sunglasses become a filter that creates innocent and inadvertent harm due to the anticipation and expectation of certain effects.

We think of prejudice as a purposeful hatred of another, but it is also a subtle filter we may be unaware of. This can reflect relationships as well, as our expectations and interpretations can create an ongoing mood change. These filters can influence our attitudes about our past, present, and future. If my filters give me the impression of hopelessness in my past, present, and future, I will feel what we call "depression."

So, you can begin to see why filters such as these cause a range of emotions, including depression, anxiety, or, on the flip side, hopefulness. Cognitive therapy considers specific thoughts, but these mental filters maybe come as preconscious or unconscious rather than conscious thoughts.

State-Dependent Memory

There is research that when we are in a certain emotional state, it is easier for the mind to recall other situations we had in that state, and harder to recall situations from other states. So, our emotions can become filters for the world.

As an example, there was a research study (that perhaps could not be repeated today) examining college students and the effects of alcohol on their exam taking. There were four groups:

1) One who studied sober and took the exam sober
2) One who studied while drunk and took the exam drunk
3) One who studied sober and took the exam drunk
4) One who studied drunk and took the exam sober

Which group did the best on their exams? This curious experiment found that those who studied sober and took their tests sober did the best. Hurrah!

The interesting part is which group did second best. It was those who studied drunk and took the test drunk. The reason is simply "state-dependent" memory. When I am in one state, I can best recall the other things from that particular state.

When we apply this to emotions, it is easy to see: When I am happy, I can best recall all the times I was happy, which reinforces my optimism. When I am sad, I can best remember all the times I was sad. I then start to build my day based on this pessimism. Notice, I am filtering the world by my own perceptions, as if it was the real state of things, rather than what I see and feel because of my own filters. It is like wearing sunglasses; we no longer see the real world, but rather the world through our filters. Unfortunately, we forget we are wearing glasses and think that our perception is reality.

Stress and the Brain

Imagine for a moment that thousands of years ago, you were walking down a path and suddenly saw a tiger. Immediately, your body stress response would begin a fight or flight response. It helps you, preparing you to run as quickly as possible or to fight the tiger.

This is the body's natural response and is lifesaving. In fact, those who had the strongest stress response lived to have children. So, over the centuries, those with a weak stress response may not have survived.

The body is very intuitive, and so this stress response adjusts things in a manner to be as effective as possible. For example, when I see a tiger, the body releases sugars and fats quickly into the blood. These sugars bring immediate energy needed to run quickly or fight the tiger in this stress response. The sympathetic nervous system also speeds the breathing, heart rate and increases perspiration.

In contrast, certain bodily systems are not as useful in this immediate urgent situation. Consequently, the body tends to slow these other systems. For example, digestion slows down. The sandwich that I just ate would not be digested for hours. I will be far away from the tiger before that becomes available for energy.

Similarly, the immune system slows down. While clotting factors are immediately needed in case of injury, the immune system is not. If I'm scratched by the tiger, it would be days before the infection would be dangerous. While reducing immunity is very effective in the context of an urgent scenario, the average American does not encounter tigers regularly. The average American stressors instead include chronic low-grade persistent stress, such as that related to work, child care, or other ongoing activities.

While these physiological stress responses are very supportive for emergency situations, it is not healthy for the body to be in a prolonged state of increased cardiovascular functioning, decreased digestive functioning, decreased immune system, or any of the other things that occur under continuing stress. Stress management in today's world is very different than the stress management that comes from traumatic events.

Bringing awareness to what types of stressors we encounter can help us to consider what types of responses would be most useful when in an emergency situation. There are limited options: typically fight, flight, or freeze. However, in my daily life, there are many options, some of which may be more thoughtful interventions for the situations I face.

For example, when I'm not in an immediate stress response, I could begin to plan ahead. I can begin to do things that will prevent the next emergency. For example, with the tiger, I could:

- Perhaps set a trap to contain the animal so that I will not have to be in that emergency fight or flight moment again
- Perhaps devise a way to deter the animal

- Perhaps move away, changing my environment, so I'm no longer near that risk

Once I remove myself from an emergency, I have a wider range of interventions available.

By managing my stress and planning ahead, I can avoid emergencies and intense emotions.

PART 2:

THE CHANGE PROCESS

CHAPTER 7

EMOTIONAL CHANGE PROCESS
▲▲▲▲▲▲ ▶▶▶▶▶

Feelings are just visitors,
let them come and go.
- Mooji

Emotions naturally change and change rapidly. In this chapter, we will explore how emotions change and consider the overall change process.

Sometimes we begin to think that a feeling is stable. I'm happy, I'm sad, or any of the other emotions we may be faced with at a particular time. This type of language suggests that the emotion is permanent and perhaps worse, it is part of our identity. But what if neither of these things is true?

We think about depression (for example) as a persistent mood state that lasts for more than two weeks. But does it really?

Try the Following Exercise:

Close your eyes and take three deep, slow breaths. Become aware of your internal thoughts, sensations, and emotions. Whenever your mind becomes distracted, return the attention to the breath. Begin to notice what happens in your thoughts over a period of two to three minutes.

A common result of an exercise like this is that you will discover a wide range of thoughts and feelings even in the course of a couple of minutes. For example, there may be a moment of anxiety as you are uncertain about what may happen next; then you may have a memory of how you are angry at your boss; followed by moments of guilt for not paying attention to your breath; or of relief or happiness that the exercise is almost over and maybe even more. Emotions can change very rapidly, just as they did with the visualization exercise from Chapter 2.

However, sometimes we get lost in our label, for example, "sad," and the familiarity of it, without realizing how sad changes as quickly as someone tells a joke, cuts us off in traffic, or surprises us with a hug. Now that we understand how quickly emotions change, the practice is about how to change how common that feeling is. Much like stress, it is not about completely getting rid of a feeling but just bringing it back to a normal level.

Feelings as Sensations versus Emotions

It is important to understand that there is an interaction between feelings and emotions. We often use these terms interchangeably, although they are a little bit different. Emotions are the moods that we use to label our experience, for example, "sad." Feelings are sensations that occur in the body.

When I feel sad, there are corresponding sensations that occur in the body. For example, in the exercise in Chapter 2, you were asked to consider what the experience was in the body during a memory. When I experience the emotion labeled sad, there are feelings in the body. For example, someone may feel a heaviness in their chest or a numbness or a foggy feeling in their head. When someone is feeling anger, they may notice tension in their jaw or hands.

Our language is filled with examples that reflect how emotions are grounded in sensations within the body, for example, heavy-hearted, light-hearted, butterflies in the stomach, light-headed, hot-headed, or many other examples of descriptions of sensations that are commonly associated with certain emotions.

> *Practice Now: Notice your current experience. Mentally scan your body to identify any current sensations. What mood would you label these sensations? Choose one of the following: Fear, Anger, Happy, Worry, Sad. Over time we will practice with a more complex range of emotions but start with just these five. Repeat this practice several times over the next week.*

Emotional Change Process

In general, the emotional change process works in three steps: 1) Identification, 2) Change of the feeling, and 3) Maintenance. We will look at each of these briefly and expand more throughout the remainder of the book.

Identification

Much like getting out of denial, the first step is awareness. Awareness itself is healing. We often think we know it all, but often our symptom is much more complex than we realized. Take some time to explore the feeling. Consider, for example:

- Where do I feel this feeling in my body? In my head? In my chest? In my belly?
- Is it a lightness or heaviness?
- Is it a tension or relaxation?
- How intense is it?
- How frequent is it?
- Is it only in certain situations?

- Does it NOT occur in certain situations?

- Does it change when I am tired or hungry?

- When did it start?

- What else was going on in my life when it started?

- Is there any context outside of myself that impacts this feeling (for example, the economy, or if the neighborhood is peaceful or distressed)?

- Is it really as I think it is, or am I misperceiving it in some way?

- How do I know it is this way?

- Are there other feelings associated with this one?

- How does this feeling relate to those other emotions?

As we work to better identify and understand emotion, we might consider using a tool such as an emotions wheel. Emotions circles list a range of emotions, arranged in certain themes, so you can review them and identify which emotion you are experiencing at the moment. Often you can identify four-to-six emotions associated with any given situation. This type of tool helps to raise awareness about the complexity of the emotional landscape. There are many examples of varying detail. This style of circle will be familiar to those with experience in Chinese Medicine. Using the circle below, see if you can identify several emotions you are feeling now. You can also download a copy from the resource page of my website at www.Dr.KenMartz.com.

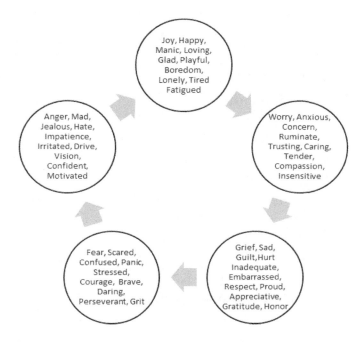

Change of Emotions

Once you identify the emotions, next comes the process of changing the feeling. There are many tools to do this. A number of these tools are discussed throughout this book. Some examples include:

- External professional support
  - o Psychotherapy
  - o Couples/family counseling
  - o Psychiatry/medicine
  - o Hypnosis
  - o Peer support group
  - o Massage
  - o Acupuncture

- o Yoga
- o Tai Chi
- o Chiropractor
- o Nutritionist
- o Personal exercise trainer
- Personal Change
  - o Journaling
  - o Letter writing
  - o Breathing
  - o Meditation
  - o Yoga
  - o Progressive muscle relaxation
  - o Changing beliefs
  - o Forgiveness
  - o Letting go
  - o Grounding techniques
  - o Visualizations
  - o Drawing/painting

I may use a range of techniques to find the one or combination that works best for me. I may also want to use a combination of personal and professional techniques. Some techniques will be designed to work very specifically on a situation (for example, letter writing to a loved one who has passed away to manage my grief) while others may be more generic, changing the mood state (breathing, exercise, and other techniques).

Maintenance

Many of these tools can quickly give short-term relief or change from a feeling state. Since emotions can become habitual, it is often necessary to repeat the tool or use other methods to maintain the changes that are obtained. These can be planned specifically for the emotion in question. For example, if I learn that I become sad every morning when I am sleepy, I can plan to have a good night's sleep and awaken with an energizing form of exercise to prevent that morning fatigue sensation I have labeled as sadness. It is also possible to create preventive practices, such as a regular exercise program, which some research has said can relieve mild to moderate depression. In creating maintenance plans, it is useful to structure helpful occurrences at regular intervals. For example, I will meditate for ten minutes every morning at 7 A.M. It is also possible to link tools to events. For example, I will take four deep, slow breaths whenever I feel the heart-racing sensation of anxiety. Maintenance can also make plans to address things before they happen. For example, if I know I become anxious when driving, I can plan to spend three minutes in mediation prior to driving.

In the coming chapters, we will explore some of these tools, more specifically as they relate to certain situations.

CHAPTER 8

AWARENESS OF EMOTIONS

To be aware is to be alive.

\- Anonymous

Consider the following:

- It is impossible to change things that we are not aware of.

- If I am not aware, any change is done *to* me rather than *by* me.

- Awareness does not always - or automatically cause change.

- In many cases, simple awareness can cause change immediately.

- If change comes from me without awareness, it will be accidental (which may help or hurt the situation)

Why is Awareness so Important?

Developing awareness is essential to effective action, particularly to intervene when problems have arisen. Deepening awareness leads to the prevention of problems before they occur. Consider the example of an iceberg. If I am aware of the tip of the iceberg, I can change course. However, the more I deepen my awareness, seeing it from a distance, understanding its depth and breadth, even under the water surface, the better I can create an effective plan of action.

Awareness Heals

Sometimes awareness alone is enough to create a change. For example, sometimes, when a baby cries, it does not need to be fed or changed. Simply being held in awareness by a loved one is enough to ease the dis-ease. Similarly, when someone is kind enough to let me know I have some spinach stuck in my teeth, I can quickly adjust.

Awareness Exercise: Changing Awareness

Sit or lie in a comfortable position and close your eyes. Mentally unplug from the world for the next three minutes. Put your awareness on the tip of your nose. Feel the temperature of the room. Expand your awareness to your breath. Notice how the breath immediately changes as soon as you begin to observe it. Now begin to notice the temperature as the breath goes in and out of the nose. Can you sense a difference in temperature from inhalation to exhalation? Can you notice the effect of the flow of breath on the sensation of temperature? As you observe the temperature, does the flow of breath (speed or depth) change yet again?

For just a moment, try to "not" control the breath and notice what occurs. For just a moment, try to control and change the breath, making it faster or slower. Do you notice what happens in your mind as you are aware of this? Are there mental judgments of how it "should" be? Is the mind "controlling" the breath or creating a verbal commentary after an experience? Explore variations a little longer before coming back to the room.

Notice how in just a few moments, there is a wide range of elements to awareness. There is a direct interaction between awareness and spontaneous change as well as purposeful change.

This is true in other areas of life as well. For example, awareness changes our experience of anger. You may have heard that saying that in retail stores, "The customer is always right." This quote is not about submissiveness or giving things away, but rather about listening. When a customer is angry, the best thing we can do is listen. Simple awareness, even without the intention of "handling" the concern, can help to ease the anger.

Often, we may complain about an issue, when we walk away, we may feel even angrier if we felt like they didn't listen or tried to prove we were wrong. Similarly, if we feel heard, even if we didn't gain a solution we wanted, we may feel more at ease.

Breathing Awareness Exercise: Observation

Sitting still with the spine tall and long, allow yourself to breathe. Notice how the breathing is now. Start to notice how the breathing is shallow or deep, fast or slow. Notice how as soon as we start to observe the breath, it changes. Continue for several breaths.

Awareness alone changes the breath. Begin to notice if you can let go of the intention of changing the breath. Begin to notice if you are able to observe the breath, like passively watching waves of an ocean. Perhaps notice if you can let go of any judgments that the breath should be faster or slower or in any way different than exactly as it is.

Increasing Awareness

When I increase my awareness, it is like shining a light on a dark space. It helps to make the situation clearer. With the light of awareness, we can have a deeper and more accurate understanding of the situation. Understand that there is also a limit to how much is needed. Just as a magnifying glass can increase our focus, it can also focus sunlight so that it burns.

Similarly, have you ever experienced a moment when a loved one criticized you? Have you then gone on to worry about that situation, repeating it over and over in your head? Perhaps telling friends about how bad this loved one is, how wrong they are for saying those words. Similarly, this excessive focus burns us with anger after the situation has long passed. In this case, the solution comes not from an awareness of hyper-focus but of broader awareness.

For this reason, it is important to increase not only the depth of our awareness but also the breadth of awareness.

Sometimes when we are lost in thought, we may not realize how that thought expresses on our face and body. While I am "stuck" in one simple piece of emotion, I may be so hyper-focused on an issue that I cannot see the solution.

There is a story of how hunters catch monkeys. They take a log and attach a chain to it, so it is connected to the ground. Next, they create a small hole and hollow out the inside. Placing a banana inside the trap, they can leave, and wait. The unsuspecting monkey comes along and sees the banana. The monkey reaches its hand in through the hole to grasp the banana. Suddenly it is trapped. As it tries to pull out the banana, it cannot get out of the small hole sideways. The monkey clasps harder and pulls harder, becoming agitated. It starts to scream in frustration, which alerts the hunter that the trap is sprung. Try as he may, the monkey cannot escape until it is released by the hunter.

We are often just like these monkeys, trapped by our firm intent on a single solution. Sometimes when our focus is intensely narrow, we cannot see that the trap is one of our own makings, and the solution is quite simple; let go of the banana. Let go of my intended goal, and I may become free to do so much more. Often, we live our lives in cages of our own emotions, unable to see the broader picture. This is yet another example of how quickly broadening our awareness can transform a situation, and ultimately our lives.

> *A human being is a part of the whole of what is called by us the universe, a part that is limited in time and space. He experiences himself, his thoughts and feeling as something separated from the rest, a kind of optical delusion of his consciousness. This delusion is a kind of prison for us, restricting us to our personal desires and to affection for a few persons nearest to us. Our task must be to free ourselves from this prison*

> **-Albert Einstein**

How Do I Increase My Awareness?

There are many tools to increase awareness in depth and breadth. Throughout this book, we will be exploring a range of them. Each exercise adds another layer of awareness. Try a range of them. Find the one or combination of approaches that resonates with you at this stage. Then practice. This will increase self-awareness.

It is valuable to have the support of someone else. I cannot see things that are in my "blind spots." These can be very obvious to others, even though it is difficult for me to see myself. For example, the situation of having spinach stuck in my teeth, as discussed earlier, makes it clear that others can easily gain awareness of something I do not know. For this reason, consider collaboration with a loved one or friend.

Consider the support of a professional counselor, another teacher, or professional, to help with the lesson you wish to learn. When I want to learn to play the violin, I can simply start to practice and can become very successful in this way. However, guidance from an expert can speed my progress considerably.

Awareness Exercises

Breathing Awareness Exercise: Abdominal Breath

Let's begin to focus on our breathing. Begin by simply allowing the breath to be exactly as it is. Begin by letting go of any judgments about how you think it should be. Placing one hand on the belly and the other hand on the chest, begin to notice which hand moves, and how. As we continue to breathe, see which one moves first and which one moves second, or if they move at the same time. Letting go of any judgments about how it "should" move or why, notice how the breathing pattern changes over the course of several breaths or minutes. Notice the breathing pattern continuing to change substantially, without any effort at this time. Simply bringing awareness to the practice.

Take a moment to begin to change the breath on purpose, exhale completely, inhale deeply into the belly, allowing the chest to remain still. Exhale by squeezing the belly in, pulling the navel in, up and under the ribs. Inhaling, let the belly drop down and out, extending open. Exhale by squeezing the belly in, up, and underneath the ribs, pressing the diaphragm upwards. Inhale by drawing the diaphragm down, which pushes the belly down and out, creating some space. Continue to breathe like this for several breaths, becoming aware of this abdominal breath movement. If you find that the chest is moving, you may try sitting against the back of a chair or lying on the floor. Continue this practice for three minutes to raise awareness of the muscles and patterns of movement for abdominal breathing.

Breathing Awareness Exercise: Meditation

Meditation is an excellent practice to build awareness and mental calm. To meditate, follow these four simple steps:

1) Find a comfortable posture and close your eyes.

2) Choose a point of focus, such as observing the breath or repeating an affirmation over and over again.

3) Continue with your awareness on that point of focus for some time.

4) When the mind wanders, gently call it back to your point of focus.

You can practice for a minute or two to start. Then eventually increase as you are able to get up to twenty minutes twice a day.

Important Resources

You can download a free handout of an introduction to breathing and meditation techniques from the resources page of my website at www.DrKenMartz.com. Audio versions of the guided meditations in this book are also available.

CHAPTER 9

EMOTIONAL CHANGE
➤➤➤➤➤➤ ➤➤➤➤➤

*All emotions, even those that are suppressed
and unexpressed, have physical effects. Unexpressed
emotions tend to stay in the body like small ticking time bombs
—they are illnesses in incubation.*
- Marilyn Van M. Derbur

There are a number of general approaches to the change of
emotions. For different individuals, different tools may be
preferred. Sometimes, if the first is not effective, additional can be
used to help feel a greater sense of mastery and control.

Beliefs

Cognitive therapy is one of the best-known, evidence-based
approaches to the treatment of mood disorders. Teaching the entire
system is beyond the scope of this text. In general, activating events
cause consequences. For example:

1) I see a snake, and
2) Feel fear.

Cognitive therapy suggests that this reaction is controlled by my
beliefs about snakes. So, the pattern is:

1) I see a snake,
2) I believe that it is dangerous,
3) I feel fear.

Notice that in this model, treatment involves identifying the beliefs and changing them. So, if I can come to learn and believe that snakes are not dangerous, I will no longer feel fear. The same applies to depression or anxiety. In this model, one must identify the beliefs that are causing the sadness and alter them to change the mood state. This can be a very effective method to directly alter the chain of beliefs that leads to the emotion we want to change.

Notice how this process begins with awareness, in this case, of specific beliefs and thoughts. Then there are ways to help alter those thoughts by identifying how the thought is inaccurate. For example, it may be black-and-white thinking (when the reality is usually in shades of gray) or "fortune-telling" (predicting the future as if it is a certainty when there is no evidence). Once you understand how a belief is inaccurate, it is possible to replace that thought with another less anxiety-producing thought, which is typically more accurate or "rational."

Is it True? Am I Absolutely Sure?

A simple tool can be to identify the thought and ask myself, "Is this true?" Often the answer is "no." This simple answer opens the door to changing that belief. Once I separate from the belief from a "fact," I can start to consider a more nuanced process of replacing that irrational belief with a better story for me.

Modern Approaches

Modern applications of cognitive therapy called Acceptance and Commitment Therapy use a meditative awareness combined with the belief change process to improve awareness and change. Meditation practices help us to:

- Increase awareness to recognize the thoughts and change them

- Develop skill in redirecting the thoughts away from such beliefs

- Create a "safe space" where I have the confidence to explore thoughts that are anxiety-provoking

Emotion

Different emotions interact with each other. This will be explored further in Part 3 of this text. For example, when I am angry, this emotion can be calmed by a respectful listening ear. Similarly, a moment of fear can be eased by a compassionate, supportive friend. There are treatment approaches, such as dialectical behavioral therapy, that focus on the role of the therapist in creating a relationship stance that balances the mood and emotional engagement of the person in treatment.

Physical

As discussed above, the body can respond physically and very rapidly to a range of emotions.

The Angry Cat Posture

Consider the image of an angry cat. Many years ago, in the wild, animals would regularly face threatening situations, including life or death fights with other animals. Instinctively they know where the most vulnerable spots are on the body. One common place is the throat, and another is the belly. Both places hold vital organs, as well as limited bone, to protect the body.

Explore your body for a moment and notice what happens if you draw your chin downwards towards your heart. You will be able to feel the chin bone naturally has a V-shape that will settle in against the collarbone, closing off the vulnerable area of the throat and creating a layer of protection for that vulnerable spot.

You may explore for a moment, also pulling your navel in and under the belly, rounding the back slightly. As you do so, you may notice that the ribs slide down, covering more and more of the belly, making that area more protected.

When you clench both the belly and the throat, notice how that also creates chronic tension in the shoulders and the back. It creates a rounded back, much like that of the angry cat. We call it the angry cat but notice that it really is about safety and protection. Like other situations, this is very effective for the cat to warn others as well as to protect itself.

This acute stress response is effective in the short term, but the chronic strain in the chest, shoulders, and belly can create other challenges for the body. It's very common in our culture to carry stress and strain in our shoulders, belly, and hips. What could be some of the effects of irritating the body in these locations for days, months, years, and decades? Would it be surprising to develop a symptom in this chronically-strained area? We call this disease, but when you begin to observe closely, you may find that it is not from an external force but a chronic internal force.

By bringing this awareness to life, we can better understand decision making that responds to the true nature of the problem. Challenges in life may sometimes be external and may sometimes be internal. The better we can identify the cause (or causes) of challenges we face, the better we will be able to define an effective response.

Physical Response

Our body has physical reactions very quickly to our changing mood states. Our breathing changes rapidly in response to our sympathetic and parasympathetic nervous systems. The reverse is also true; changes to the body can alter our mood. Sometimes something as simple as changing the physical posture can alter the mood state. Sometimes more vigorous activity such as exercise can not only change body chemistry for twenty-four hours but also can relieve mild to moderate depression and other unwanted mood states.

Another element of physical change involves eating. Every food we eat influences the body. Caffeine energizes, sugar spikes energy before a crash, healthy fats hold off hunger differently than vegetables, and various other effects are seen from other foods. Put simply, if I put 93 octane gas in my car, it runs differently than on 89 octane gas, and very different than it would on diesel or maple syrup! The fuel we give our body can affect our mood, increasing or decreasing energy levels.

There are a host of physical illnesses that can cause or complicate mood disorders. These should be evaluated by a trained medical professional. These could include issues such as diabetes, hyperthyroidism, hypothyroidism, heart disease, digestive illness, and a host of other illnesses. Managing these conditions can alter mood states dramatically.

Imagery

Similar to the cognitive approach, consider that for many people, we think not only in words and sentences but also in pictures. Neurolinguistic programming is an approach that suggests we study the people that possess the qualities we want to have. For example, we can study successful people to determine patterns in how they think or study happy people to determine patterns in how they think. As we understand their ways of achieving success, we can better make changes to get there ourselves.

One of the things that are clear is that emotions are experienced as more intense when the mental imagery of the situation is larger, closer, and more vivid, and less so for images that are smaller, further away, and vaguer. So, if I am afraid of snakes, I may imagine them as being very close and very large. This can be reduced by mentally sending the image far away. Mental changes of perception, such as these tend to remain, even though this type of intervention takes very little time.

Social Experience/Culture

Our moods occur in the context of our relationships within our family circle, circle of friends, neighborhood, and country, as well as circles of professional associations, gender associations, and racial- or cultural associations. While we place emphasis on our personal experiences, it is important to remember how our past, as well as our present relationships, anchor us into certain patterns. Changing myself can create ripple effects that are supportive of my relationships or could cause me to change relationships. For a simple example, if I have a severe alcohol use disorder, and all my friends drink at the bar with me each night, when I want to change my drinking patterns, what will happen? It will affect my circle of friends, and they will influence me as well. If we remain friends, those relationships will change.

Every time I personally change, it is connected to changes with everyone in my social circles.

Blockage to Emotional Change

At times we may feel "stuck," unable to make a change. Over time we will be exploring two ways to address this issue. First is that we may need to address our personal experience through a different modality, trying different interventions for the body, beliefs, and emotions. Next, we may need to examine more broadly to find other causes and maintaining elements, such as the roots of these beliefs in our past, our relationships, and cultural experiences over decades.

Sometimes awareness will immediately change behavior. With more ingrained issues, we may need a deeper awareness or different tools to disconnect from the structures that have maintained that emotional pattern in our life.

CHAPTER 10

MAINTENANCE OF EMOTIONS
❧❧❧❧❧ ✦✦✦✦✦

*Talent is a pursued interest. Anything that
you're willing to practice; you can do.*
- Bob Ross

Once I do the work of getting back on track, my task changes to the maintenance of the things I have learned. The old experiences will try to pull me back.

Practice

Practice starts with focused attention. The first time I try this new behavior, it may feel odd. I may make mistakes. I may need to run through the behavior with awareness and purpose, just like it takes initial awareness and effort to turn the direction of a car. Later there is still some effort, but it is much more minimal effort to maintain the practice once it is established.

Much like learning our times tables, the longer we practice this new behavior, the more ingrained it becomes, and the easier it is to continue. So, on the first day (or days), I may need to be very careful to practice. After a week, I may be into a routine. They say we need to practice about twenty-one days to develop a habit, though mastery may progress over a lifetime. We never stop getting better, some of this is life work, but in the meantime, as we improve, it is getting easier and easier.

Notice how with repetition, that memory will become more ingrained in the brain, so it will become more and more normal and easy. Eventually, it will be on autopilot, so there may not need to be any conscious effort to maintain it.

Some may say that they have made New Year's resolutions every year, and they always fail. So, let's consider how to plan for a practice that will be most likely to take hold.

Building a Practice

If something is important enough to build a practice, then take the time to do it in detail. Take a moment to consider the meaning of your practice. A practice is taking on a particular way of being, doing, or speaking. It is typically something that shows up in everyday life. This process can be broken down into four steps:

Step 1: Purpose of the Practice

Understanding the "Why" will help you to maintain motivation. Some examples are:

- It calls us to a larger purpose
- Forwards our own life
- Forwards the life of everyone around us

There may be many other specific reasons we can add, such as "to be happy," "to feel free," or "because my baby girl gets upset when she sees me sad/angry or scared." Find a "why" that is big enough to motivate you through, even on the days when you want to take a shortcut. (Hint: this also means stop reading now until you find your purpose. Continue only after you complete this step of the practice creation).

Step 2: Develop the Form of the Practice

Now that you know a clear motivation for your practice, you want to create something using the following five parts model:

1) I [declare]
2) for the sake of [whom]
3) I will [practice]
4) and remind myself by [reminder]
5) with support from [whom]

Part one begins with a declaration. This is not a half-hearted attempt. This does not begin with words like try or hope. This is a clear affirmative statement such as "I say that." "I declare that." or "I intend that."

Part two suggests at least one person other than myself who will benefit from this practice. This should be someone you care for, such as my daughter, my spouse, my dog, my sister, or a friend or co-worker. This is not just a name, but making it clear that this practice you are taking on affects multiple relationships you have. On the days when you feel lazy, this is also someone you will need to be able to look in the eyes and help motivate you.

Part three is the form of the specific practice. Be clear, concise, and very specific. For example, "I will write three things for which I am grateful in my journal every night before I go to bed for thirty days."

Part four is to add reminders. We are human with a pattern of other behaviors that are working against us. This practice is new. So, add reminders to snap us out of our autopilot and back into the completion of the practice. Some examples could be:

- Writing using a purple pen
- Sticky notes
- Wearing my watch on my other wrist
- Setting alarms on my phone.

There is a special kind of reminder that relates to the awareness of feelings in our bodies. For example, if I am working on my anger, I may be reminded to "take three deep breaths every time I notice my jaw is clenched." If I am working on developing courage, I may "remember two accomplishments, every time I notice the butterfly sensation in my stomach."

Part five involves engaging in a partnership. Who can you ask to help you with this? How can they help you? Think of a specific person, but not the person the issue is specifically for. Then speak to them. Explain what you are trying to do, what you need from them, and how they can help. For example, "Joe, I am tired of being anxious at work. So, I am starting a practice of exercising three days a week for the next month to reduce my stress. Would you join me at the gym once a week, or check in on me at least once a week to see if I am on track?" Notice that this sets up a situation where Joe may be joining you or sets up a situation where you know that the next time you see Joe, you may be responsible to report on your progress or lack of it. Having an audience for what you are doing helps keep you on track.

Step Three: Checking In

Once you have begun your practice, you'll want to set a specific way to monitor how it is going. It may be that you will journal about your progress every Saturday or discuss it with your partner every night. You may find that at the end of the week, you were successful, so you'll want to give yourself credit for that. Or you may find that you were not successful. Perhaps this is not because you did badly, but rather that the plan you made was not right for you. Use this time to revise your practice plan as needed and start again. For example, perhaps the sticky note fell off, so you needed a different reminder. Perhaps you got angry with your partner, so you stopped practicing to spite them. By setting aside this specific time to check-in and course correct, we are allowed to be imperfect, but we get closer and closer to success along the way instead of thinking of it as a failure.

If there are challenges, it may also be important to consider if the practice gets at the root cause. For example, perhaps the practice might be better to address another aspect of emotion, belief, imagery, or relationship pattern to achieve the desired goal.

Step Four: Consequences

While having a detailed plan is often enough, there are many ways to play. You can add rewards for success. For example, "If I go to the gym three days this week, I get a piece of my favorite chocolate on Sunday." You can also add negative consequences. For example, "If my partner catches me not having completed my practice, I will buy them a dinner at their favorite restaurant."

Examples:

Here are some examples of some practices to get started:

- I want to practice developing my awareness.
    - ○ I declare, for the sake of Mary (my sister), that I will look at my emotions circle at least once a day and

identify at least four emotions I experienced during the course of the day. I will remind myself by putting a sticker on the back of my watch, so I will remember when I take my watch off at the end of the day. I will ask Jane, my spouse, to check in with me to keep me active and journal about my progress every Sunday evening. If I am successful, she will rub my feet for ten minutes. If I am not successful, I will rub her shoulders for ten minutes.

- I want to develop happiness
  - I will, for the sake of Josie, my one-year-old daughter, write in my journal three things I was successful with over the course of the past day and one goal I can accomplish in the coming day. I will remind myself by setting my journal next to my alarm clock, so I will remember to do so as soon as I wake up in the morning. I will ask Jane, my best friend, to check in with me and help me remember other successes, and discuss with me how I am progressing every Saturday morning over coffee. If I am successful, I get a cookie (or *cookies*) to go with it. If I am not successful, I buy a cookie for Jane.

- I want to reduce stress at work
  - I shall, for the sake of Jack, my co-worker, take one deep breath and smile before each time I answer the phone. I will remind myself by adding a post-it note on the phone. I will ask James, another co-worker friend who often calls me, to support me by asking how I am doing and discussing with me how I am doing over lunch on Fridays. If I am successful, he buys lunch. If I am not successful, I buy lunch.

If/Then Tools

Another effective approach is to use specific steps in an If/When/Then format. This links specific behaviors to other specific events. For example, many times we say something like: "I am going to exercise three days a week," which is good but limited. It is better to say something very precise such as:

- *If* I eat ice cream, *then* I will go to the gym on the same day.

- *When* I am coming home from work Monday, Wednesday, and Friday, *then* I will stop at the gym.

- *If* I get angry, *then* I will take three deep breaths.

- *When* I feel my fists clenching, *then* I will take three deep breaths.

PART 3:

MANAGING SPECIFIC
EMOTIONS

CHAPTER 11

FIVE ELEMENTS OF EMOTIONS
➘➘➘➘➘➘ ➚➚➚➚➚➚

We each reflect the same sun. The sun shines down,
and its image reflects in a thousand different pots filled with
water. The reflections are many, but they are each reflecting
the same sun. Similarly, when we come to know who we truly are,
we will see ourselves in all people.
- Amma

In Chinese Medicine, there are five key energies in life. By observing nature, we can begin to learn about ourselves since we are a part of nature.

Seasons of Life

Let's explore a cycle of life together to see what lessons can be learned. Consider the following story:

A farmer awakens in the dead of winter. It is cold. The entire year lay before him with all the possibilities. This includes *fear*: "Will there be enough food to survive until the spring thaw?"

As time passes, the farmer awakens to early spring. It is warming, and he is able to begin his plans for planting. He is able to work hard to plant the crops and create his *vision* and reach toward his goal. All around, the seeds have the strength to reach deep to the earth for strength and push past obstacles to reach for the sun.

As time passes, the farmer awakens to summer. As the crops grow, it is warm out, so the children go out for fun and celebration. Friends can come together in *partnership and joyful play.*

As time passes, the farmer awakens to late summer. As the heat and humidity build, he begins to slow. It is the time of harvest, with the great abundance of Mother Earth's *compassionate sharing.*

As time passes, the farmer awakens to autumn. As the trees begin to lose their beauty, they are *letting go* of that which is unnecessary. The farmer stocks what is precious and needed for the winter. As nature finds its precious core center that is left behind, it lets go toward a winter's rest and renewal.

Just as nature travels through a cycle of birth, renewal, and decline, we cycle through these same emotions and patterns in a similar order. Fear of all the possibilities leads to drive and joy of success. Accomplishments are compassionately shared before being let go with sweet sadness to make room for the next adventure. Each of these will be examined in the next five chapters.

Our Emotional Nature

If indeed we are a part of nature, then consider what it means for our emotions. Can our fear lead to the drive to be successful? Can our success be celebrated and let go, making room for the next cycle?

If nature moves in a certain direction, what if our emotions also build upon one another, as an interconnected web, rather than as independent experiences?

Some may have picked up this book because of an "anger problem." Consider that perhaps the prominent emotion is not the only one out of balance, but rather the symptom of an imbalance in the entire system of emotions. While there are tools to work with anger, it may also be important to examine the fears that lead to anger and develop the skills to let go, relieving some of the accumulated anger.

In the coming chapters, we will examine each of these five emotions individually, but remember that they are each a part of a whole, interacting with each other. In the last chapter of this section, we will revisit how these emotions interact in the context of love.

CHAPTER 12

COURAGE AND FEAR
〜〜〜〜〜 〜〜〜〜〜

Fear is the path to the Dark Side. Fear leads to anger.
Anger leads to hate. Hate leads to suffering.
- Yoda

Never take someone's feelings for granted because you never
know how much courage that they took to show it to you.
- Anonymous

Exploring Fear

Imagine for a moment something you are afraid of. Something that stops you in your tracks. Perhaps it is a fear of spiders, fear of failure, or fear of success. Ask yourself the following questions:

- Where do I feel this emotion in my body (e.g., Head, chest, belly)?

- What does this sensation feel like (e.g., Heaviness, tightness, relaxation)?

- How fast does this feeling arise?

- How long does this feeling linger once activated?

- When is the first time I ever felt this emotion?

- Are there things that make this emotion more or less intense?

Fear and Courage

Fear is a core emotion. It is deeply rooted in the brain in the basic fight or flight response, so it can be seen as an activating feeling that charges motivation. It is like gas in the car, giving the strength to move. Whatever I am afraid of, having fear in moderate amounts will keep me active, focused, and motivated.

Consider fear as the shadow side of courage. It is like the front and back of my hand; one does not exist without the other. Courage is not the absence of fear, but rather the willingness to take action despite my fear. Over time I have discovered I am afraid of many things in life. By pulling our fears out of denial and into the light, I have also found that the scariest things are not real, but rather only in my imagination.

As we claim our fears, they are transformed into courage. Just like an ocean wave is scary since it can knock us off balance, in the summer, people spend hours at the beach, empowered by standing strong as the waves pass us by. Some take surfboards and other supports to master the waves from above. Our delicate balance of fear and courage creates exhilaration. Consider also roller coasters, our first kiss, public speaking, and so many other things where that initial fearful anticipation is overcome.

An example can be seen in the power of water. It is fluid and humble, seeking stillness. It manages obstacles by simply going around them, using one of the many possible paths to its goal rather than being frozen by a single obstacle.

Lack of Fear

If I never had any fear, I would quickly die since I would engage in risky behaviors such as walking in front of traffic, standing near ledges of tall buildings, or using illicit substances. Just as a lack of fear is dangerous, an excess of fear has serious risks, in addition to being uncomfortable.

Fear protects us. It keeps us out of thoughtless danger. Suppose I got my wish of having "no fear," I would quickly die because I impulsively made dangerous decisions. This can be as simple as changing dinner plans (four times in a row) or as risky as running out into a street without looking to see if a car is coming, marrying someone I met that day, taking a "shortcut" through a dark, deserted alley at night, or getting into a car with a stranger who has rope and duct tape in the back seat.

Excess of Fear

An excess of fear can "freeze" us, afraid to move forward or experience life. When a deer becomes fearful and freezes in the middle of the road (instead of running away), it is in serious danger. When overloaded with fear, I may never leave the house, afraid that the car will crash, a bee will sting me, a snake will jump out of the bushes, a person will assault me, and on and on. This is the type of experience many people think of when they consider fear. However, every act of courage and heroism is a moment of overcoming fear.

Similar to stress, fear should not be too little or too much. As we find balance, we can maintain the strength and motivation of courage, without the painful extremes of fear.

Is Fear a Familiar Feeling?

Ask yourself:

- Where are some areas that I feel "stuck" in life?
- Is there something that I want to do but am afraid to do it?

- Is there a part of my life that has become cold and boring?
- Is there a part of my life that has become impulsive and fast-paced?
- Do I have frequent regrets over quick decisions?
- Have I lost relationships because I am not reliable?

What am I afraid of (it may be more than one thing)? Review the following sample list of fears and rate each in the range of zero through 10, with zero meaning no fear and 10 being intense, immobilizing fear.

__Fear__	__Rating (0 to10)__
Success	
Failure	
Trust	
Loss of something valuable	
Dying alone	
Relationships	
Being embarrassed	
People laughing at me	
Making a mistake	
Losing	
Winning	
Getting "fired"	
Lack of money	
Someone being angry	
Partner leaving me	

Government control	
Spam cyber attacks	
Identity theft	
Disease	
Snakes	
Heights	
Spiders	
Darkness	

Obviously, the list is endless. You also consider that fear doesn't have an "on/off" switch but a range. If I ask myself whether I am afraid I spiders, I may say "no," but it may be a fear of 1 or 2 out of 10. Exercises like this can help us to increase awareness of our range of fear.

Ways to Balance Fear and Courage

There are a number of strategies specific to the management of fear, in addition to other techniques from throughout this book. Some very effective tools we have discussed include:

- Deep breathing with a focus on long, slow exhalations to relax the body, activating the parasympathetic nervous system

- Visualizations where we shrank the mental images of the feared objects

- Belief changes such as identifying what my fearful beliefs are (e.g., the snake is dangerous) and altering them.

In addition to some prior tools, we can add some new ones.

Exposure

One tool to manage specific fears involves exposure. However, the fear we experience should be manageable, so we create very low-level experiences of the fear to inoculate, build tolerance and courage to easily manage what was previously an intolerable fear.

This tool is best if I am afraid of something specific, for example, snakes. Begin by creating a list of scenarios that you are progressively fearful of. Next, rank them with numbers ranging from 0 to 100. For example:

- 0 A book about the history of snakes on a table in Canada
- 10 A book about snakes on a table at my neighbor's house
- 20 A small pet snake in a cage at my neighbor's house
- 30 A small pet snake in a cage in my house three rooms away
- 45 A small pet snake in a cage in my house in the next room but not visible
- 55 A small pet snake in a cage in my house in the next room, and I can see it
- 67 A small pet snake in a cage in the next room with the cage door open
- 75 A small pet snake loose in the room
- 85 A small size snake near my feet
- 95 A small size snake crawling on me

You may have other examples or substitute for other types of issues like fear of heights. Begin by using your favorite stress reduction, such as deep breathing, then imagine the first image. You may notice a slight fear response. Continue to breathe until that response fades, then increase to the next image. Continuing one after the other, taking breaks as needed until more and more fearful images no longer create a stressful fear reaction.

Just do it.

For certain fear responses, taking action is critical. If I am frozen in fear, simply taking one step forward can interrupt the cycle and help with a breakthrough. For example, if I am afraid to ask someone out to dinner, the simple act of taking the next step can reduce the fear. Get the phone number and dial the phone. If I am paralyzed in fear for ten minutes waiting to make the call due to fear of rejection, then I will have a period of discomfort. The longer we wait, frozen in fear, the more we experience the discomfort. Why wait twenty minutes when I can call immediately and have a resolution, one way or the other. Paralysis prolongs the discomfort, so take a step toward action.

Grandmother Hug

Imagine your beloved grandmother, aunt, or teacher, giving you a big hug and standing with you as you face the fear. Choose someone you know has confidence in you. Find the proper image for you, and let their strength support you.

Courage Builder

Consider what the worst thing that could possibly happen is. Consider how likely (or typically unlikely) that could occur. Knowing the feared outcomes and how unlikely they are can help to have the strength to overcome them. Over time, developing trust that we are safe makes it easier to take healthy risks.

Affirmations

Say some of the following quotes to myself. Repeat often.

- I am strong.

- I am courageous.

- I am flexible/adaptable.

- I trust.

Yoga Pose: Cobra

Lie on your belly and bring your hands under your shoulders. Palms are on the floor with fingertips reaching to underneath the top of your shoulders. Using back strength, gently raise your head and shoulders, feeling the heart lifting up and forward. You can also push the hands gently into the floor to raise a little higher but continue to use your back strength as your focus. Hold for three breaths, lower down to rest. Repeat as often as you like.

The cobra requires us to have the strength of courage to rise up from the ground, able to protect ourselves and face the fears before us. As you practice, visualize and feel the strength of courage.

Visualization

Lie down in a comfortable position and close your eyes. Allow the body to melt into the ground as the breathing softens over several breaths. Imagine you are in a theater watching a movie where you are the hero, having just overcome your fear. See how you are standing in the movie. Notice your shoulders, your face, and your eyes. Now step out of your chair and walk up to the movie screen.

Walk into the screen and step into the place where you are in the movie. Notice what it feels like in your body to stand in this way, knowing you were able to overcome your fear. Searching your memory, you can see the steps of how you overcame this fear, with clarity on how easy it was. Take a few breaths to savor this feeling of success as it soaks into every cell of your body. After some time, allow your fingers and toes to wriggle, awakening with this clear sense of self to carry with you into the day.

Practice

We can practice doing things that scare us. Doing so over time can help build our courage. Consider practicing the following to practice overcoming "safe" fears:

- Take a new exercise class
- Try a new hairstyle
- Smile at someone
- Start a brief conversation with the grocery checkout staff
- Try a new hobby
- Rearrange your furniture
- Wear something in your closet that you never do
- Try a new flavor of ice cream
- Go to a new restaurant
- Try something different on the menu than your "usual" meal
- Turn off the TV for one day
- Pick a random channel and watch it
- Drive a different route to work
- Cook a new recipe
- Tell someone a secret
- Ask someone for help
- Admit something you don't know
- Take "the road less traveled"

Take a Moment to Reflect

Take a moment to reflect on what you have been learning. See where you are at now:

- Is fear a bad thing?
- Can I begin to be aware of the physical sensations in my body that I label as "fear"?
- If I am afraid, is it a temporary feeling state?
- If it is temporary, which tools work best for me?
- Are there things that make the fear worse for me, that I should avoid?
- Can I imagine myself strong and full of courage?
- Can I hold an image of myself as strong and full of courage for two minutes?
- What if I could hold this strength and courage for one day?
- Knowing I am strong and courageous, what can I do to help remember this easily and continuously?

Is this the same or different than you were experiencing before? Continue to notice changes in your experience of fear and courage as we discuss anger and drive. Consider how courage helps give us the motivation to act, which becomes our inherent drive, or anger.

CHAPTER 13

DRIVE AND ANGER
❥❥❥❥❥ ❧❧❧❧❧

*Don't hide your feelings. Act on them. You never
know when that chance will no longer be there.*
- Anonymous

*Anger is the feeling that makes your mouth
work faster than your mind.*
- Anonymous

Exploring Anger

Imagine for a moment something you have been angry about, such
as something that caused a sudden and sharp frustration. Perhaps it
is someone who cut you off in traffic, annoyance at something a
loved one said this morning, or anger at your boss for asking you to
work late today. Ask yourself the following questions:

- Where do I feel this anger in my body? (e.g., Head, chest,
  belly)

- What does this sensation feel like? (e.g., Heaviness,
  tightness, relaxation).

- How fast does this feeling arise?

- How long does this feeling linger once activated?

- When is the first time I ever felt this emotion?

- Are there things that make this anger more or less intense?

Drive and Anger

Drive is the vision that gives us direction in life. It offers motivation to achieve our goals. We associate it with successful people who are able to know what they want and take effective steps to achieve their goals. This includes the strength to "power through" fatigue, challenges, and obstacles. It is similar to the strength of a tree, which reaches deep into the earth and far upward toward the sun. Rocks that get in the way are pushed aside so the tree will reach its goals.

In excess, this drive is what we call anger, aggression, or rage. It is a painful emotional state, like the animal that lashes out after being wounded. This level of emotion can be damaging to us and to those around us, creating fear in those who experience it.

If I lack this drive, I will become a passive pushover. I may internalize my anger, judging myself for perceived weakness and cowardice. When I am not clear about what I want in life or do not use my courage to take steps to realize those goals, it can leave me feeling weak, unfulfilled, and inadequate.

What Makes me Angry?

There may be many things that make me angry or frustrated. What are some of the ones that are particularly annoying for you?

Disappointment	Failure
Unmet expectations	When someone is late
"Bad" drivers	My boss
My spouse	My child
People who don't hold the door for you	Restaurants that charge for refills of soda

People who don't respond to a text immediately	Slow internet
Poor customer service	Telemarketers
Bullies	Power outage
Spam email	People talking loudly on their cell phones

Tools to Work with Anger and Drive

Breathing

One of the most well-known interventions for anger is breathing. Start with a slow deep breath. Allow the exhalation to be about twice as long as the inhalation. Count to three or four as we inhale, and count to six or eight with each exhale. Repeat until the feeling softens.

Decisions/Solutions

Often anger can relate to a frustrated goal. Instead of being focused on our frustration and what we are lacking, we can turn our focus toward solutions to the issue. For example, if I am frustrated about a spam email, I can do many things. Identify some and begin one, for example:

- I could change my email address.
- I could examine spam filters.
- I can change the spam settings of my current email provider.
- I can add my name to federal spam lists.

Identify Underlying Beliefs/Expectations

The anger that we experience has roots in our thoughts. Consider what some of the beliefs are that I hold that cause my anger. For example, if we are angry at a "bad" driver, perhaps we have beliefs such as:

- He/she is "stupid"
- They "should have"...[been more cautious, looked first, or done something differently]
- They are "making" me late
- I could have been hurt

When we can understand the specific belief that causes our anger (*should* statements are common here), we can begin to change them. When we adjust our expectations, the anger eases.

Physical Exercise

Exercise is a rapid way to change our emotional state. It immediately changes the speed of our breath. It detoxifies stress-related chemicals. It releases tension from the body and makes hormonal changes that last up to twenty-four hours. As a culture, our lives have often become more sedentary. When we lose our physical strength and regular activity, it diminishes our strength to manage crises. Consider how our mind tries to trick us into stopping our exercise. The practice of exercise includes the skill of pushing past our limitations, one more minute, one more repetition, one more set, one more pound, or one more of whatever it is we are working at.

Planning

Planning is the process of identifying our triggers of anger and planning around them. It involves looking ahead to prevent flare-ups of rage. It also involves making sure that our vision and drive do not fall too low and become apathy or passivity.

While we think of anger management as "calming down," this is really about intervening in a moment of anger. When a pot boils over on the stove, we need to calm the temperature quickly, but it is important to know how to prevent the overflow. Whenever possible, it is best to develop a plan for anger prevention. With the boiling pot example, we may consider:

- Were we paying attention?
- How much water was added?
- How much food was added?
- How long were we cooking?
- Did I have the flame on high or low?
- Was the lid on?

The framework of these questions about boiling water can help us consider ways to change the situation. Let's see how this framework applies to the anger at a "bad" driver scenario by considering the following:

- Were we paying attention, allowing us the most advance notice of their "bad" behavior? Or were we distracted, thinking about something, drinking a soda, changing the music, talking on the phone, yelling at a child in the back seat?

- How much water was added? Am I heading to the appointment early, on time, or late? A rushed attitude can affect my anger risk.

- How much food was added? Do I drive defensively or aggressively? Do I drive close to the person in front of me, or leave space?

- How long were we cooking? When I am tired and fatigued, this can impact not only my reaction time but also my irritability. As fatigue increases over time, it can also increase my risks

- Did I have the flame on high or low? To an extent, I control the mental pressure and drive with which I approach life. Do I live a relaxed, slow-paced life, or a rushed daily race?

- Was the lid on? Certain things cause pressure to build rapidly. Do I carry anger like a collection, or am I able to "ventilate" by letting go of prior anger so that they do not build?

Journaling

Writing our thoughts in a journal or on paper can also be helpful. The process of writing can slow the racing mind. Writing can move the angry thoughts out of our head onto paper, creating some "mental distance" from them. Once written, we can also rip – up the paper and throw it away, or otherwise dispose of the thoughts somehow, "releasing" them, rather than carrying them internally.

...And What Else?

I often say that anger is a false emotion. As we become aware of our emotional landscape, anger is almost invariably covering over another emotion(s). Typically, it is hiding fear. Simply asking the question "and what else" can help us to identify these other emotions that hide underneath. The use of a tool such as an emotions circle can also help us to scan emotions to find others that are hiding. For example, with the case of the "bad" driver, underneath my anger often lies a flash of fear of danger when we slam on the breaks. Identifying the underlying emotions will also help to "vent" the anger, by diminishing it at the root, just like turning down the flame under the pot of boiling water.

Assertiveness

As we calm our anger, we can gain more clarity and direction for solutions. Anger is typically a request in disguise. If I can develop an awareness of the situation as well as what I am thinking/feeling, then I can better identify what solution would help that situation. For example, perhaps I cook a delicious dinner for my spouse. The table is set as they are late coming home from work. The food is getting cold, and I become angrier with each passing minute. As I become clear of the scenario and my emotions, I can create more specific solutions for the future. For example, we could plan to eat out. We could plan dinner time later to allow cushion time for traffic or delays. We can agree to communicate about delays like traffic. Of the many solutions, we can choose one and regain control, rather than feeling victimized.

Affirmations

Say some of the following quotes to myself. Repeat often.

- I have a clear vision for my life.
- I can ask for what I need.
- I can negotiate when I have differences with others.
- I have the drive and strength to achieve my goals.

Yoga Posture: Tree Pose

From standing, shift all of your weight to your left foot. Turn the right foot to point to your right side with the heel on your left ankle. If this is enough, remain balancing as much weight as you can on your left leg. If you are stable, there is an option to slide the right foot up the left leg to the calf. You may then also bring your hands together to prayer posture in front of your heart. If you are steady, you can also "grow branches" reaching your hands straight to the sky. Continue for three breaths before slowly lowering back down to standing and practicing on the right leg.

The Tree pose is a practice of assertiveness. We begin by planting our foot firmly rooting into the ground. We feel the stability of our base before eventually growing branches, reaching for the sun, identifying our goal in life, and having the strength to reach for it. Trees sway. There is a gentle flexibility in trees, so they are neither passive nor aggressive, but hold a stable assertive balance. As you practice, feel the strength of reaching for your goals and maintaining balance in life.

Visualization 1

Lie down in a comfortable position and close your eyes. Allow the body to melt into the ground as the breathing softens over several breaths. Imagine you are in a theater seeing a movie where the situation you are watching is causing you to be angry. Notice the words and posture of the characters. See the movie's vivid color. Ask yourself how intense is the anger on a scale of one to ten.

Expand your awareness to see the edges of the screen. Then imagine the screen shrinking to television size. Let the image become dull and turn to black and white. Perhaps a silly theme song plays behind the image. Finally, let the television move farther away, far off into the sky and into space. Ask yourself again how intense the anger is on a scale of one to ten, noticing how quickly it has lessened. After some time, allow your fingers and toes to wriggle, awakening with this clear sense of freedom to carry with you into the day.

Visualization 2

Lie down in a comfortable position and close your eyes. Allow the body to melt into the ground as the breathing softens over several breaths. Imagine you are in a theater watching a movie where you are the hero. With the clarity of vision, you see your goal and understand the steps to achieve it. See how you are standing in the movie. Notice your shoulders, your face, and your eyes. Now step out of your chair and walk up to the movie screen. Walk into the screen and step into the place of yourself. Notice what it feels like in your body to stand in this way, trusting your ability to apply your knowledge to follow through to effective solutions. Standing tall, you can see with clarity the next steps, with clarity on how easy it is. Take a few breaths to savor this feeling of success as it soaks into every cell of your body. After some time, allow your fingers and toes to wriggle, awakening with this clear sense of self to carry with you into the day.

"Venting" our Anger

"Venting" is a tricky situation. It seems a commonsense approach to relieve pressure. But the way we do so may or may not be helpful.

Some suggest "venting" our anger by doing things such as punching a pillow, beating my spouse with a foam stick, going to a private space and screaming, going to the back yard to do a chore, such as chopping wood.

As we consider the potential value of such approaches, let's replace the term "venting" with "practice." Venting anger sounds like a good thing. However, but if we "practice anger" by punching, hitting, or screaming, it may not have the intended effect. What happens when we practice things? They become more common.

For this reason, we may want to consider alternatives to practicing these behaviors. Instead, we can practice breathing, exercise, journaling, and other helpful modalities. In a later chapter, we can also use a tool called "forgiveness."

Practice

We can practice having the clarity of mind to know what we want and the planned steps to achieve our desires. Doing so over time can help build our assertiveness. Consider practicing the following:

- Practice a weight training exercise, such as pushups
- Identify a goal and list three steps to achieve it
- Mentally map the turns on your way to a location
- Practice listing three wants and three needs in your life
- Write a "to do" list for the day and prioritize what you put on it

Take a Moment to Consider

Pause a moment to reflect on what you have been learning about anger and drive.

- Is anger a bad thing?
- Can I begin to be aware of the physical sensations in my body that I label as "anger"?
- If I am angry, is it a temporary *feeling* state?
- If it is temporary, which tools work best for me?

- Are there things that make anger worse for me, that I should avoid?

- Are these things the same or different as those who can help me with my fear?

- Can I imagine myself as strong, driven, and focused?

- Can I hold an image of myself as strong, driven, and focused for two minutes?

- What if I could hold this strong, driven, and focused image of myself for one day?

- Knowing I am strong, driven, and focused, what can I do to help remember this easily and continuously?

Is this the same or different than you were experiencing before? Continue to notice changes in your experience of anger and drive as we discuss boredom and joy. Consider also how drive causes us to complete actions. The completion of actions can lead to the joy of feeling successful.

CHAPTER 14

JOY AND BOREDOM
➦➦➦➦➦➦ ➥➥➥➥➥

Let anyone who comes to you go away feeling better
and happier. Everyone should see goodness in your face,
in your eyes, in your smile. Joy shows from the eyes. It appears
when we speak and walk. It cannot be kept closed inside us.
It reacts outside. Joy is very infectious.
- Mother Teresa

Exploring Joy

Imagine for a moment something you have been joyful about, such as something that caused a sudden and intense moment of happiness. Perhaps it is the birth of a child, a wedding engagement, being accepted at a college/job, or simply the freedom of dancing at a party. Ask yourself the following questions:

- Where do I feel this emotion in my body (e.g., Head, chest, belly)?

- What does this sensation feel like? (e.g., Heaviness, tightness, relaxation)?

- How fast does this feeling arise?

- How long does this feeling linger once activated?

- When is the first time I ever felt this emotion?

- Are there things that make this emotion more or less intense?

Joy and Boredom

Some may have skipped ahead to this chapter to learn how to be happy. Everyone wants this flavor of ice cream, this particular spice of life. It is also one that is more elusive. In earlier chapters, you may have easily thought of moments of fear or anger, but was it also easy to think of a memory of joy?

Like other emotions, this occurs in a range. Sometimes we may initially think of joy in terms of very rare events such as the birth of a child or getting married. These are very useful to get the initial feeling sensation. Once you are clear of the feelings, it is easier to broaden our awareness to other times with a similar sensation and emotion.

Joy or happiness is common when we experience success in life. This may be accomplishing a task, winning a game, or kissing a loved one. It is also often associated with a feeling of playfulness and connection with others.

Lacking Joy: Boredom

Lacking this feeling in life leads to feelings of boredom and loneliness. Boredom is a lack of pleasure. It is possible that your situation is truly boring, but most often, this is either:

1) A lack of awareness
2) The stifling effect of grief and sadness
3) The freezing effect of fear

For each of these issues, you can also see the other chapters on those topics for further consideration.

Excessive Joy: Mania

At first, one may think it is impossible to have too much joy. In psychological terms, this is called "mania" or bipolar disorder. In this case, individuals experience an intense and persistent mood state, which can be very challenging. This is often accompanied by a range of impulsive behaviors.

What Helps me Feel Joy?

As we build awareness, consider which of the following you enjoy:

Games	Tickle fights
Dancing	Pillow fights
Massage	My favorite ice cream
Kittens	Chocolate
Jokes	Sunsets
Hugs/kissing	Ocean waves
Completing tasks	Fridays
Spending time with friends	Movies
Spending time with kids	Running
Spending time with parents	Jazzercize
Other_____	Other_____

There are many books and websites of 1,000 things to be happy about. Find your personal pleasures. Consider a range of playful and active choices, and plan to do some regularly.

Tools to Work with Boredom and Joy

Clearing Grief

As we relieve our fear and grief, we will be better able to find joy. The work of those chapters will support your practice of joy.

Smiling/Laugh

Smiling triggers the part of the brain that helps us to feel happy. It is easy to do and to repeat. It can boost the immune system and relieve stress. It is also said to relax dozens of muscles across the body. Laughing or whistling a song are also effective tools to explore.

Massage

For many people, touch feels good. Explore massage chairs, partner massage, or professional massage as options to practice these feelings. There are many good books or videos to teach basic massage so you can exchange massages with your loved one. There are also many different techniques used by professional massage therapists, which not only feel good but also relieve stress and tension.

Breathing

As discussed, breathing is one of the fastest ways to change the feeling state of the body. To explore an energizing breath, allow yourself to inhale to a count of six and exhale to a count of three for several breaths. This shift in breath pattern can be energizing, just like the body yawns when feeling sleepy.

Affirmations

Say some of the following quotes to myself. Repeat often.

- I am successful.

- I celebrate success.

- I have trustworthy partners in life.

- I enjoy "playtime."

Yoga Posture: Dancer

From standing, shift all of your weight to your left foot. Bending your right knee raise the foot up behind you. If you are comfortable, reach your right hand back to hold the foot. The left hand reaches up toward the ceiling. The heart lifts up and slightly forward, creating a slight curve in the back. If this is enough, remain there. If you are comfortable with more, begin to kick the foot backward while the heart leads, leaning forward. Continue for three breaths before slowly lowering down and practicing on the right leg.

Dancer pose is a practice of lighthearted joy. We begin by planting our foot firmly rooted into the ground. We feel the stability of our balance ease as we stretch forward and back. The dancer is a practice of opening the heart to play. There is a flexibility of the dancer that opens us up. While we may not be able to hold the balance as long, there is a feeling of accomplishment of the achieved beauty, which is magnified by its impermanence. As you practice, feel the lightness of being, the freedom to dance.

Visualization

Lie down in a comfortable position and close your eyes. Allow the body to melt into the ground as the breathing softens over several breaths. Imagine you are in a theater watching a movie where you are the hero, with the pride of having saved the world and are receiving praise from the city. Perhaps you share this moment with a loved one. See how you are standing in the movie. Notice your shoulders, your face, and your eyes. Now step out of your chair and walk up to the movie screen. Walk into the screen and step into the place of yourself. Notice what it feels like in your body to stand in this way, savoring the joy of successful accomplishment. Standing tall, you can feel the lightness of being able to accomplish whatever comes next. Take a few breaths to savor this feeling of success as it soaks into every cell of your body. After some time, allow your fingers and toes to wriggle, awakening with this clear sense of self to carry with you into the day.

Practice

We can practice the attitude of play and success. Doing so over time can help build our sense of happiness and joy. Consider practicing the following:

- Play a game with a five-year-old

- Read a joke book

- Watch a funny movie

- Make up a game to play with your spouse or loved one

- Make funny faces at someone

- Laugh at yourself

- Laugh like you mean it

- Smile at everyone you meet today

- Turn on your favorite song, and dance like no one is watching

- Turn on your favorite song and dance with a loved one

- Check things off your "to-do" list

- Make a list of three things you accomplished today, this week, this year.

Take a Moment to Consider

Pause a moment to reflect on what you have been learning about joy and boredom.

- Is joy a bad thing?

- Is chasing joy/success a good thing for me?

- Can I begin to be aware of the physical sensations in my body that I label as "joy"?

- If I am joyful, is it a temporary *feeling* state?

- If it is temporary, which tools work best for me?

- Are there things that make joy more muted for me that I should avoid (for example, guilt, worthiness, fear)?

- Can I imagine myself strong and full of happiness?

- Can I hold an image of myself as strong and full of happiness for two minutes?

- What if I could hold this strength and happiness for a whole day?

- Knowing I am strong and happy, what can I do to help remember this easily and continuously?

- Knowing strength and happiness are "who I am," why would I ever give that up?

Is this the same or different than you were experiencing before? Continue to notice changes in your experience of joy and boredom as we discuss compassion and insensitivity. Consider also how success causes us to want to share.

CHAPTER 15

COMPASSION AND INSENSITIVITY
\\\\\\\ //////

*Research has shown that a simple act of kindness directed toward
another improves the functioning of the immune system and stimulates
the production of serotonin in both the recipient of the kindness and
the person extending the kindness. Kindness extended, received, or
observed beneficially impacts the physical health and feelings of
everyone involved.*
- Wayne Dyer

Exploring Compassion

Imagine for a moment something you have been worried about,
such as something that caused a sense of concern and rumination
about a situation. Perhaps it is a worry for the health of a child,
worry about finances, or how to "make" your loved one appreciate
you. Ask yourself the following questions:

- Where do I feel this emotion in my body? (e.g., Head, chest,
  belly)?

- What does this sensation feel like? (e.g., Heaviness,
  tightness, relaxation)?

- How fast does this feeling arise?

- How long does this feeling linger once activated?

- When is the first time I ever felt this emotion?

- Are there things that make this emotion more or less intense?

Compassion and Insensitivity

Compassion is an emotion that can be overlooked but is often a core desire. Consider, for example, the father who wants his daughter to marry a "nice" "sweet" guy, a stable rock to be there through the challenges of life. This speaks to a core element of relationships in which we support one another. These are also included in common marriage vows "for richer, for poorer, in sickness and in health," which speak to the commitment to tend to one another as challenges arise over time. This emotion is grounded in feeling the strength of my own center so that I can support others, just as a mountain offers shelter and trees offer fruit. Compassion fosters gifts freely given of our time and our heart. These are the gifts of the holiday seasons, which can sometimes be forgotten since they cannot be bought in a store and wrapped in a box.

Insensitivity: A Lack of Compassion

At times, in this high-paced world, we can become so busy that we become self-focused on my house, my job, my phone, my car, and other examples of "my" things. When there is a lack of compassion in the world, there is an increase in many social ills that are seen as "other people's problems," like poverty, illness, depression, substance use, homelessness, and hunger.

Excessive Compassion

While we perhaps cannot be too "open-hearted," excessive compassion can be painful and damaging in relationships. Consider what happens to children that have "everything they want." As a parent, it can be difficult to say "no" at times. It hurts to deny them their desires, although it is most loving to set certain boundaries, for example, "No, you cannot have a third piece of cake instead of dinner."

Another example of excess can be seen as worry. We all have an "Aunt Tessie" who lovingly worries about us, offers ice cream when we visit. If we refuse, then she offers cake. If we refuse, then she offers candy. This type of imbalance can leave one depleted since it is from "giving it all away," rather than sharing like the candle shares its light and heat.

What Helps me Feel Compassion?

We can raise awareness of compassion in our lives by considering what causes me to recognize that feeling of "Awww," and the related desire to help our loved ones. Consider some of the following:

Bandaging a child's "boo-boo"	Holding the door open for someone
Making chicken soup for a sick child	A welcome gift to a new neighbor
Commercials for abandoned animals	Leaving a note in your child's lunchbox
Commercials for hungry children in another country	Bringing doughnuts or lunch to share at the office
A friend asking for "help"	A warm smile
Seeing a baby	Snuggling with a pet

Tools to Work with Compassion

Touch

While being sensitive that some individuals may prefer not to be touched, doing so can quickly communicate this emotion. Different than touch for pleasure, as we discussed in the previous chapter, this touch is about communicating connection. A bear hug, a pat on the back/arm, or holding someone's hand can quickly communicate this sense of "I've got your back," or "I'm here with you."

Donating

Donating communicates to ourselves and to others that I have abundance and can share freely. Some spiritual traditions encourage sharing in this way, known as "tithing." While this is commonly a donation of money, we can also donate our time, expertise, or other things. Many of us have children's toys that have been outgrown, clothes we no longer wear, or other things that can be donated to local programs. Donating to others is also a gift to ourselves since it feels good for us to be helpful.

Volunteering

This shares of ourselves and can engage the heart. Volunteering at a children's hospital, a soup kitchen, or other such places can help us to connect with this sense of compassion. There are many ways to volunteer that may be one-time events or become regular traditions.

Gifts Freely Given

Sometimes people "keep score" with gifts. Practice an attitude of the gift freely given, not as competition or to "get" something.

Often when I give freely, I also get things in return, but giving is not for that purpose.

Exercise

Physical exercise of various sorts is an excellent way to get "out of our heads." It forces attention into the body and into action rather than simply "spinning our wheels." Exercise with an aerobic practice and our favorite music can be particularly helpful, creating short-term attention, as well as a calm that comes after the more intense exercise.

Journaling

Journaling is a great way to not only express our thoughts, but it requires us to slow the thoughts enough to be able to write them out. The practice of writing them can also interrupt the cycle of mental rumination. Mentally we may repeat ourselves, but we tend not to do so in writing.

Grounding Techniques

Many quick tools can be used to increase our sense of worry or anxiety. These simple tools bring a moment of attention to the present moment. For example, feeling the temperature in the room on your skin, feeling the weight of your body supported by the ground/chair/bed, counting the yellow objects in the room, noticing the smells in the room, or small sounds we usually don't hear, like a fan or children playing outside nearby.

Breathing/Meditation

Breathing is an excellent tool for calming worry. The simple focus on the exhalation and focus on the physical body can help quiet the mind. Like a snow globe, just being still for a period of time, like the stable mountain, can help to quiet the internal storms of life.

Affirmations

Say some of the following quotes to myself. Repeat often.

- I am stable and solid despite challenges.
- I have all that I need.
- I have enough that I can share, supporting others.
- I am compassionate and warm-hearted.

Yoga Posture: Mountain Pose

From standing, keep your arms at your side. You may turn the palms to face slightly forward, helping the shoulders to broaden open. Be here now. Be aware of major muscle groups. Pressing the feet into the ground can engage the calves. A gentle tense in the upper thigh will adjust the hip. We can lift tall out of our waist, expanding our abdomen. Lifting tall will encourage the heart to lift and open, spreading the chest and shoulders broad. The top of the head lifts slightly by slightly pulling in our chin, elongating the back of the neck. Breathe here for several breaths.

Mountain pose is a practice of stability and compassion. Mountains stand tall and strong. As storms pass through life, mountains will not be moved. The mountain may provide shelter to others; it also causes water to run away and collect into a place where animals can get a drink. The nourishment of the Earth provides food, sharing without fear of scarcity. The strength of the mountain is not how it imposes its will on others but that it stays stable and reliable. Mother Earth is always there beneath our feet, supporting us. As you practice, feel the strength of stability and compassion running through you.

Visualization

Lie down in a comfortable position and close your eyes. Allow the body to melt into the ground as the breathing softens over several breaths. Imagine you are in a theater watching a movie where you are the hero, with the balance to know who you are and where you stand in life. That stability attracts others to you like a shelter from the storm. See how you are standing in the movie. Notice your shoulders, your face, and your eyes. Now step out of your chair and walk up to the movie screen. Walk into the screen and step into the place of yourself. Notice what it feels like in your body to stand in this way, confident in where you stand in life. Feeling abundance, it feels safe to give to others freely, sharing your strength. Standing tall, you can simply trust how easy it is, knowing that you are perfect as you are, even as life continues to evolve and change. Take a few breaths to savor this feeling of stability and compassion as it soaks into every cell of your body. After some time, allow your fingers and toes to wriggle, awakening with this clear sense of self to carry with you into the day.

Practice

We can practice having the clarity of mind to know what we want and the planned steps to achieve our desires. Doing so over time can help build our compassion. Consider the regular practice of the following:

- Be still and breathe
- Feel the weight of your body supported by the Earth
- From seated or lying down, relax my muscles, noticing how the more I do, the more the Earth immediately supports me.

- Volunteer at a children's hospital or soup kitchen
- Give a gift of time to someone
- Help someone who needs a hand
- Share a good meal with someone
- List three things in your life that you have plenty of, just for today.

Take a Moment to Consider

As you explore this range from insensitivity to worry, think about that balance of compassion:

- Is worry a bad thing?
- Can I begin to be aware of the physical sensations in my body that I label as "compassionate"?
- If I am worried, is it a temporary feeling state?
- If it is temporary, which tools work best for me? (e.g., effective action or decision making) ?
- Are these the same or different tools that help me with anger?
- Are there things that make worry or anxiety more intense for me that I should avoid?
- Can I imagine myself strong, full of stability and centeredness?
- What if I could hold this strength, full of stability and centeredness, for one whole day?
- Knowing I am strong, full of stability and centeredness, what can I do to help remember this easily and continuously?

Notice also how compassion naturally gives rise to respect. When I give to someone, the most common response is, "Thank you."

CHAPTER 16

RESPECT AND GRIEF

*If I choose to bless another person, I will always
end up feeling more blessed.*
- Marianne Williamson

*If you are carrying strong feelings about something
that happened in your past, they may hinder
your ability to live in the present.*
- Les Brown

*When we think that God is with us, all our burdens
will be lessened. Once we have entered a boat or bus, why
should we continue to carry the luggage? Put it down.*
- Amma

Awareness of Sadness and Grief

Imagine for a moment something you have been sad about, such as something that caused a sudden and perhaps intense moment of loss. Perhaps it is a time when a relationship ended or a financial loss. Ask yourself the following questions:

- Where do I feel this emotion in my body (e.g., Head, chest, belly)?

- What does this sensation feel like? (e.g., Heaviness, tightness, relaxation)

- How fast does this feeling arise?

- How long does this feeling linger once activated?

- When is the first time I ever felt this emotion?

- Are there things that make this emotion more or less intense?

Respect and Preciousness

Consider the importance of respect and values in our lives. Knowing what is important lets us prioritize so we can remain sharp and effective. Prioritizing also helps us to let go of less important things. Understanding our self-worth helps to keep us centered when challenges occur.

Lack of Respect: Devaluing

Sometimes we may feel devalued or unimportant, or communicate that to others. This often leads to anger due to feeling offended by a perceived injury. The experience of "nothing matters" is one face of depression.

Excess of Respect: Grief

In contrast, we can hold something so precious that its loss causes grief, or we hold on beyond the time we should. When there is a death or loss of relationships, it is normal to feel that loss. It is a deep respect for the gift that existed in that relationship.

Sometimes, we can "hold on," resisting the change even when it is time. Much like hoarding can be problematic, there are situations when items have completed their time. When I purchase and eat a can of soup, the empty can is no longer needed. It is time to take out the trash, but delaying can cause it to become stagnant and foul. In relationships, we do not "throw people away" but take the best of the relationship and memories with us as we move forward, letting go of the rest.

What Helps Me Feel Respect?

Over the course of our day, there may be many things that activate this emotion. Consider some of the following:

Saying "Thank you"	Receiving help from someone
Someone thanking me	Someone saying "good job"
Grace before meals	Asking before taking other people's things
Various prayers	Remembering birthdays
"Quitting time" at work	Rewards
Letting go of the day to drift off to sleep	Smiles

Tools to Work with Respect and Sadness

Values Clarification

Explore and identify my priorities across a range of areas of life. What criteria are important for you? What types of things do you want to include in life to be more rounded or more fulfilled? You can sharpen this with specific overarching values and smaller steps to implement those values.

Needs versus Wants

Among our list of desires, group them into needs versus wants. Needs are things that we must have to survive, such as oxygen. Wants are icing on the cake that we would love to have but are not "deal breakers." In dating, for example, we may "want it all" but understand the difference in priorities.

Writing a Letter/Burn It

Simply writing out our experience can help externalize it. In this exercise, give yourself the freedom to write the fear, anger, or hurts that you are uncomfortable to say but are "stuck" thinking about. This expression can help you to "let it go." Plan that whatever is written is to be burned (releasing it) or otherwise destroyed so that you can safely express a range of difficult thoughts or emotions and experience your freedom from it.

Breathing

You may notice breathing appears as a tool for working with a number of these emotions. It is one of the most diverse tools. In the context of grief, exhalation is about "letting go." We tend to hold our breath in grief, so easing our breath can help to break that cycle.

Spirituality/Religion

While not everyone identifies with a specific religious or spiritual tradition, those who do can find the sacred in the context of their practice. Rituals, prayers, and connecting with something larger than ourselves can stabilize this feeling of honor.

Gratitude Journal

Similar to writing in general, we can start a gratitude journal. Each night, we can write down three-to-five things we are grateful for from the day. This list practices and focuses our attention on gratitude, and over time, develops a strong list to anchor and remind us on the days when we forget our worth.

"I'm sorry."

Apologies can relieve and interrupt anger in others. It also helps us ease and clear our own guilt about past mistakes. When apologizing, we may ask for forgiveness, but understand we are not responsible for anyone to forgive us.

Forgiveness

Often, we need to forgive ourselves or others for past hurts. Forgiveness is not about them; it is about us. Consider, for example, the individual who steals your wallet. They have moved on and may never see you again, but we may carry the hurt, fear, and anger of the wound. Just like people die not from the snake bite but from the poisonous venom left behind, our anger is like poison. Forgiveness is about clearing our own anger, not the other person's guilt. Note this does not mean they cannot be held accountable for their actions, only that I don't carry that pain any longer. Forgiveness is about freeing *ourselves*.

Affirmations

Say some of the following quotes to myself. Repeat often.

- I am valuable.
- I respect those around me.
- I know what is most important to me.
- I am deserving and worthy.

Yoga Posture: Knee Down Twist

Lie down on your back. Bending your right knee into your chest, clasp the knee with both hands, giving it a gentle hug. Release the right hand and reach it along the floor to your right side. The left-hand guides the knee to the left as far as comfortable. Your right hip may rise off the floor but keep both shoulders flat on the floor. Continue for three breaths before slowly unwinding and practicing on the other leg.

Knee down twist is a practice of drawing inward to the preciousness of our core. Opposite of the tree that actively reaches open, knee down twist is like the autumn, letting go of the foliage, to remember our core self. As we relax into the pose, all the muscles in the body stretch away from our core, wringing out any unnecessary tensions that we carry. As you practice, feel the strength of reaching for your goals and maintaining balance in life.

Visualization

Lie down in a comfortable position and close your eyes. Allow the body to melt into the ground as your breathing softens over several breaths. Imagine you are in a theater watching a movie where you are the hero, with the value and self-respect to trust yourself and the confidence to let go of all that is unnecessary. See how you are standing in the movie. Notice your shoulders, your face, and your eyes. Now step out of your chair and walk up to the movie screen. Walk into the screen and step into the place of yourself. Notice what it feels like in your body to stand in this way, confident in your core. Trusting the value in the center of who you are, when all else falls away. Take a few breaths to savor this feeling of respect as it soaks into every cell of your body. After some time, allow your fingers and toes to wriggle, awakening with this clear sense of self to carry with you into the day.

Practice

We can practice having the clarity of mind to know what we want and the planned steps to achieve our desires. Doing so over time can help build our respect and ability to "let go." Consider practicing the following:

- Clean out the "junk drawer"
- Donate some old clothes to make room for new things
- Take out the trash, even before it is full
- Find one table and make it into a Zen surface
- Identify your number one priority and make a picture representing it to place on your bathroom mirror
- Look at yourself in the eyes in your mirror
- Look at yourself in the mirror and smile
- Say "Thank-you" to three people today.

Take a Moment to Consider

As we have explored a range of techniques surrounding grief and values, consider:

- Is grief a bad thing?
- Can I begin to be aware of the physical sensations in my body that I label as "grief"?
- If I am feeling grief, is it a temporary feeling state?
- If it is temporary, which tools work best for me? (e.g., letting go, visualization)?
- Are there things that make shame worse for me that I should avoid?

- Can I imagine myself strong and full of self-respect?

- Can I hold an image of myself as strong and full of self-respect for two minutes?

- What if I could hold this strength and self-respect for one whole day?

- Knowing I am strong and full of self-respect, what can I do to help remember this easily and continuously?

Consider also how letting go creates space for new possibilities. This can be frightening, as we complete the circle of emotions back to where we began. While this circle of life continues, perhaps there is something else, a container for it all?

CHAPTER 17

GETTING TO LOVE

A human being is a part of the whole called by us universe, a part limited in time and space. He experiences himself, his thoughts and feelings as something separated from the rest, a kind of optical delusion of his consciousness. This delusion is a kind of prison for us, restricting us to our personal desires and to affection for a few persons nearest to us. Our task must be to free ourselves from this prison by widening our circle of compassion to embrace all living creatures and the whole of nature in its beauty.

- Albert Einstein

One Ring to Rule Them All

When we experience a "negative" emotion, we may become focused there. You perhaps selected this book because a certain emotion was calling for your attention. In recent chapters, we explored these concerns directly. Now let's step outside those concerns to find the larger environment that holds those emotions.

For some, we may call this larger perspective: love, neutrality, balance, Higher Self, or some other term. For this section, I will be using the term "Love."

In the words of the old song, "Life is but a dream," but who then is the dreamer? Who is the "self" experiencing all these emotions? When I connect with this higher perspective, things change.

Emotions as Calls for Love

This range of emotions we have been exploring are all warning signs when something is wrong. What if every complaint or upset in our lives is a call for help, a call for love? Sometimes those calls arrive in a sweet voice, and sometimes they are harsh, but all bring us closer to some higher sense of balance. When I see them as such, it is easier to let go of judgments and engage more fully.

When a child whines, we can hear it through eyes of judgment or hear it as begging for help, even though they cannot clearly articulate some unmet need.

The range of emotions are motivators calling us back to center when we are lost. They are warning signs when we are going in the wrong direction. Perhaps we can begin to see them as friends rather than enemies, within this larger context.

Nothing is Constant but Change

Emotions are constantly changing since there are many rhythmic changes in life; there are the cycles of the day, of our biology, even of the seasons. Imagine standing at the edge of the ocean for a moment. There is a constantly changing push and pull as the waves come in and go out. The shifting pressures can knock us off balance, or cause our feet to bury deeper in the sand, becoming more rooted and stable over time.

Just as shifting sands polish rough edges, the ebb and flow of life's journey helps to polish us, deepening our understanding of life. We must constantly shift to keep up. From this perspective, dis-ease exists where we did not shift along with the required changes in life. Dis-ease is the place where we refused to yield to the changes that were needed.

Continuing the ocean example, we can consider that the turmoil is most present at the surface and the edges. It is possible to go deeper into the ocean. Deep beneath it all is a great strength and stillness, just like the center of a spinning top is balanced.

We Have Two Eyes, but One Vision

We have two eyes that see things differently. It is not that one is right, and one is wrong. Instead, we have one larger Vision, which encompasses it all. Just the same, emotions are not "good" or "bad" but parts of a whole, with a share in its purpose.

What Helps Me to Experience Love?

Perhaps it is not about starting or stopping a particular emotion but learning to savor the balance of the dance. When we stop fighting the dance, we can settle down to find our center. There are many paths to this center. Choose whatever combination works for you. There are no wrong paths, although some may be more direct or faster than others.

- For some, we may choose a religious or spiritual connection to create a "homing beacon" to guide us closer to this center.

- For some, we may choose to hold close to our beloveds. These intimate relationships can help create a safe space to model and be the center of this love in a tangible way in our lives.

- For some, we may choose a path of personal exploration. For example, a deep meditation practice explores our way to this sense of higher consciousness.

Once we experience it, things become easier due to the deep sense of knowing. For example, once I see the sunrise and know that it occurs daily, whether or not I see it, there is no longer any turmoil of doubt.

Some think that one becomes "enlightened" as if it is a destination. While perhaps this occurs for some, it is perhaps more common to experience moments of enlightenment. Once we experience even a very brief moment of this sense of love, it becomes a deep knowledge that persists and frames our future understanding. This is a common experience of individuals who have experienced "near-death" moments and reorient their lives with a new sense of passion, often focusing on new priorities of importance.

Moving Forward

To this point, we have emphasized our personal experiences of emotions. In Part 4, we will explore further to consider how this applies to our relationships and the world around us. These simple principles within us are maintained within our relationships with those around us. As we become clearer about our internal experience, we will be more skillful in applying this skill in external relationships.

PART 4:

EMOTIONS APPLICATIONS

CHAPTER 18

EMOTIONS AND MOTIVATION
〰〰〰〰〰

Attitude is a choice. Happiness is a choice. Optimism is a choice.
Kindness is a choice. Giving is a choice. Respect is a choice.
Whatever choice you make makes you. Choose wisely.
- Roy T. Bennett

Don't be pushed around by the fears in your mind.
Be led by the dreams in your heart.
- Roy T. Bennett

Motivation is closely tied to emotion, like the gas in the engine. Just like stress, if there was no motivation, we could never get out of bed in the morning. Without motivation, we would wander around aimlessly. Everyone is motivated, but we may or may not be aware of what we are motivated for. Consider for a moment that if I am not aware of my motivation, it will be driving me perhaps to an area which is not what we truly want.

Ask myself:

- Am I aware of what motivates me?
- Can I list three key motivators in my life today?
- Am I often motivated to escape harm?
- Am I often motivated to achieve a specific success?
- Have I experienced a failure and did not know why?

- Are there ways I have been motivated to failure rather than success?

- Are there ways I have been motivated to stay the same rather than change?

- What beliefs do I have about motivation and success?

- Where did I develop these beliefs from in my past?

- Do I feel able to achieve the things I want?

- Do I feel worthy of achieving the things I want?

Avoidance/Attraction

Often there are two core motivators: Avoidance and Attraction. While I have multiple motivations for different situations, often, these fit into one of these two categories. Avoidance reflects a motivation to be away from pain, danger, or harm. Attraction is motivation toward something I desire, enjoy, or want.

Avoidance Motivation

Avoidance motivation is critical to maintaining our safety and security. These are often associated with basic human needs and often associated with fear. I may avoid a range of things:

- Afraid of someone becoming angry/violent

- Afraid of being hurt

- Afraid of losing (competition)

- Afraid of loss of relationships/abandonment

- Afraid of loss of money

- Afraid of judgments from self/others

- Afraid of admitting a belief that I am not "good enough"

- Afraid of exposing a "secret"
- Afraid of success

Notice the themes of danger vs. safety. For many people, it is difficult to think about long-term goals because I am dealing with short term, very real dangers and risks. For example, it can be difficult to think about how to be successful at work while I am worried about paying the bills. It is difficult to think about how to have a strong partnership relationship when I am afraid of my partner becoming angry and yelling or assaulting me.

Fears can create a laser focus on that issue. When I am standing in front of a tiger, I am not worried about other things in my life. Unfortunately, this can also blind us to effective action in this specific situation.

Even though it is difficult, it can be valuable to step back to think of both my long-term goals, as well as these short-term safety goals. I may want to get quickly out of the frying pan, but don't want to jump into the fire. Looking ahead to my goals is important, so this initial motivation out of pain can motivate us closer to a long-term goal.

Attraction Motivation

In contrast, there can be things we are motivated for because we *want* them. Once our basic needs are met, we can begin to examine long-term needs and wants, such as:

- Want to feel courage
- Want to feel drive/passion
- Want to feel financial stability/abundance
- Want to feel successful

- Want to feel happy
- Want to feel a deep connection with my loved one
- Want to feel respected
- Want to "love myself"
- Want to feel deeply loved by another
- Want to have it all

As we consider this list is there any one of these goals that we do not want? Notice how attractive motivation can be. It can be overwhelming because we "want it all," and we deserve it. With attractive motivation, sometimes the issue is prioritization. We need to consider which one is most important first, second, and third. Also, which one will "unlock" several others, so it may gain higher priority since it leverages success.

Motivation and Miracles

Let's explore these motivations a bit more with the following visualization. Please choose one of the attractive motivations from the list above to explore deeper. For teaching purposes, I am going to use a motivation for courage, but feel free to substitute your personal goal or repeat this exercise with multiple goals.

> *Sit or lie in a comfortable position and close your eyes. Imagine moving forward in time to bedtime tonight. Set a clear intention and wish to feel strong and courageous in all that you do. As you fall into a deep, comfortable sleep, you are able to relax and let go of any barriers that held you back in the past. Suddenly, a miracle happens, and you are granted deep courage and confidence. However, you are still asleep, so you do not yet know this has happened. As you awaken again, what with be the very first clue that something has changed? How is life experienced differently with this newfound courage? What happens next*

in your morning routine? What happens next that surprises you into realizing, "something is different today." How many of these surprises occur before you realize that the change occurred in you? What happens next that confirms for you that this change has occurred? Take a moment to savor this feeling in your entire body. When you are ready, wriggle your fingers and toes and return to the room you are in. Slowly opening your eyes with a new way to see the miracles in the world today.

What do you notice during this exercise? Perhaps upon awakening, you noticed a different sensation in your body. Perhaps you spoke a little differently to your loved one or coworker. Perhaps you still did many of the day-to-day routines but did so with a different emotion.

Sometimes our attractive goals seem so far away, but they can be achieved even today. Subtle shifts of emotions, mood, and interactions can be miraculous, creating a "whole new world." This type of newfound confidence can help make it easier to address an avoidance motivation that seemed impossible at the time. Once we know where we are headed, it is easier to find the path that connects the dots from our present to that future.

Stress as Motivation

Stress is a fear-based motivator. It can protect us from harm or risks if we can maintain a balance.

Motivation Exploration

Imagine waking up in the morning, lying comfortably in bed. You may find that since it's comfortable, you choose to linger a little longer. You feel warm and safe and may choose to linger a little longer. After an hour or two, you begin to notice what happens next. Changes start to occur. Perhaps you need to use the restroom or become hungry. Perhaps you begin to have judgments of yourself for being lazy. In response to these internal pressures, we get out of bed, and we begin activities.

Next, you go downstairs to get the food, and the refrigerator is empty, so perhaps you need to go to the grocery store. You go to the grocery store and suddenly realized that your wallet is empty, so you need to get back to work. You get back to work and realize you're dissatisfied with your job. So, you find a new job or higher-paying job or an additional job. And so on...

Stress is usually perceived as a bad thing. But it isn't always. Stress is pressure that builds. It causes us to get out of bed in the morning. We need stress to be active and productive.

However, when stress becomes too much, I can begin to feel overwhelmed, overloaded, and become much more ineffective. The modern way of thinking about stress is not that we need to get rid of stress. Rather, we need to find stress management. Like Goldilocks, we need not have too much stress or too little stress.

We want to be at that peak performance at the highest level of activity. Consider how to balance the amount of stress at that peak.

Advanced Motivation

Like other areas of this book, this chapter is merely an introduction. If you want to deepen your understanding of motivation, consider applying issues from each of the other chapters as well. For example:

- Where did I develop my beliefs about motivation?

- What beliefs do I hold about motivation?

- Do I know I am able to change my motivation quickly and easily?

- Am I aware of my motivations at work?
- Can I apply my attractive motivations in my relationship/family life?

Motivation and emotions are the fuel that we use to grow in all areas of life. We are always motivated and growing. These are simply tools to raise awareness of our motivation so that we can begin to apply it more effectively on a daily basis.

CHAPTER 19

EMOTIONS AND COMMUNICATION
❦❦❦❦❦ ❧❧❧❧❧

You can talk with someone for years, everyday, and still,
it won't mean as much as what you can have when you sit in front of
someone, not saying a word, yet you feel that person with your heart,
you feel like you have known the person forever... connections are made
with the heart, not the tongue.
- C. JoyBell C.

Miscommunication is a common source of tension in relationships and can impact our success in many ways. When our communication is unclear, we can inadvertently hurt other's feelings or feel frustrated ourselves.

Types of Interactions

To begin, let's consider how communication falls along a spectrum, rather than an on/off switch. It may range from passive to aggressive.

Passive <---------------Assertive-------------> Aggressive

With passive communication, I may not be clear about what I want to communicate. If I don't know, then it is safe to say the communication will not come across clearly. When I don't get my needs met, I can become sad, depressed, or irritable, which can also be frustrating to those around me.

With assertive communication, I am aware of my needs, and I communicate them clearly. This is a balanced communication since the listener may or may not respond. This style tends to earn respect since it also gives respect to my companions.

With aggressive communication, I am aware of my needs and communicate them clearly, just like assertive communication. The difference is that there is an expectation that the communication will be fulfilled. It may go as far as a direct or implied threat. This is intimidation and may get the need met. However, it is a losing strategy since it is very uncomfortable for those around us, and they will leave, making it more difficult to achieve future goals.

Types of Communication

Our interactions can be broken into specific types of verbal communication such as requests, ranging from in the extreme from passive complaints to active demands.

Passive <---------------Assertive-------------> Aggressive

Complaint <-------------Request-------------> Demand

Complaint

Each type of communication has a certain communication style. Passive communication may include silence or complaints. An example of a complaint may be: "It is so hot in here." Notice that there is no clear solution to this type of communication. It is whiny and reflects feelings of dissatisfaction. It is not known if this individual wants me to open a window, adjust the air conditioning, get a glass of ice water, or move the discussion elsewhere.

As an assertive listener, it is up to me to clarify. For example, "Yeah, it is hot today, is there something we could do to help with that?" Notice this question does not take responsibility for fixing the problem. This question is simply clarifying the concern and helping the individual articulate a more specific request.

Request

Assertive individuals use requests. In this case, the response could be, "It is so hot today. I would love a glass of water, could you get one for me please?" Notice how this is clear and specific communication. If you ask several people this question, most will say yes, and some may say no. There is also a third response, which is a return request, such as "Not right now since I am still watching this TV show, but I can get it for you during the next commercial?" Notice we are now in the negotiation of counter-offers. This respectful dialogue continues until someone either agrees or says "no."

Conditions of Satisfaction

Assertive requests also include clear conditions of satisfaction. It is my responsibility as the requestor to be clear how I would like the request fulfilled. If I do not ask for it, I share responsibility for the lack of fulfillment of the request. For example, "Thanks for getting me this glass of water, but I really wanted cold ice water." Again, as the listener, it is our responsibility to be clear about what we are agreeing to.

It is important to determine and communicate the conditions of satisfaction along with the request. So again, we could simply have asked, "I'd be happy to get you a glass of water. Would you like ice with that?" At the extreme, the requestor could ask, "Could I please get a glass of water, right now, a large 32-ounce glass with three ice cubes. It should be Evian water that was chilled in the refrigerator overnight and have one slice of lemon." Clearly, this can be taken to an extreme, which makes it more likely the listener will say "No." Somewhere in the middle is clear communication.

Demand

The third type of communication is the demand of an aggressive individual. In this type of communication, there may be a clear request. However, there is an expectation that there is no denial or counteroffer. As an assertive person, we can simply say "no" if we choose to, although we may face some negative responses, so we may need to choose our response carefully for the short-term. Longer-term, we may choose to limit contact with such a person.

"I" Statements

It is useful to use statements that start with "I" rather than "you." We are assertive in labeling our emotions. I feel sad. I feel hurt. I feel frustrated. In contrast, "you" statements can be threatening and accusatory, for example, "You made me mad." They did not make you mad. We do that all by ourselves, based on our beliefs and emotions of our accumulated history.

Consider the white male who is insecure about his weight but confident in his mathematical ability. If someone becomes angry and screams at him, "No wonder you are so fat and lazy." Since he has an internal vulnerability to this issue, he may feel scared, angry, and hurt. In contrast, if someone yells at him that he "is stupid and probably doesn't know what 2+2 equals," he may be more apt to ignore the insult since he experiences no vulnerability in this area.

"I" statements are intended to seek help and minimize accusation. "You" statements risk attacking at a vulnerable spot in the partner, escalating the situation.

Emotions and Assertiveness

As just described, assertiveness requires neutrality to maintain a balanced approach. Consider also the effects of emotion on assertive communication. Fear can cause a person to become frozen and passive. It can also unleash an intense emotion that will be perceived as a demand. Similarly, if I speak with a tone of angry emotion, it will be presented as a demand. On the other hand, compassion can do the reverse. It can weaken me into passivity since I don't want to impose. It can also make a request seem aggressive, like a mother bear protecting her cub.

Our range of emotions can complicate clear communication. When possible, we should address them in order to communicate better. However, often communication is part of the process for addressing the wounded emotion.

Words Matter

There are a number of words that should be stricken from our vocabulary, never to be spoken again (with perhaps a couple of rare exceptions like learning them in this chapter). Every time we use these words, suffering happens, either within ourselves or in our relationships. This can undermine our communication and create relationship conflicts.

"Should" "Ought" "Must" "Have to"

Using words such as these immediately creates guilt, anger, and helplessness. For example:

- "I should have been on time,"
- "You ought to be on time."

"Should" and "Have to" statements convey a conflict of feeling dragged into something against my will in the future. For past events, it creates nothing but shaming for something that cannot be changed. There are only two things in life that we truly "have to" do: 1) Die, and 2) Live until then. All the rest are choices.

Instead of "Should" and "Have to" statements, consider replacing with "Value" or "Want" to create freedom of choice, for example:

- "I value punctuality."
- "I know you want to present a good impression by being on time."

Notice how this simple shift in words feels more empowering. Another common example is that I don't "have to" do this task at work. I want to have a job, and I value not getting fired, so I choose to do this task to the best of my ability.

"Can't"

This is typically inaccurate, and creates dissent. For example:

- "Would you join me for a cup of coffee?"
  - "No, I can't."
- I can't solve this puzzle

Very often can't is simply untrue. Are you *able* to drink a cup of coffee? Yes. It is more accurate to say that you are choosing not to do so, perhaps for some other reason.

There is a range of ways to replace the word "can't." It can be replaced with "I won't" "I refuse to," which are less socially polite, but accurate and empowering.

It is possible to simply delete this word entirely, for example:

- Would you join me for a cup of coffee?"
    - "No, thank you."

Depending on the situation, "can't" may also be replaced with "not yet." There was a time when we did not believe we could fly. If Orville and Wilbur Wright (the first to fly a plane) believed that we couldn't fly, we might still be on the ground today.

In the puzzle example, is it true that I "can't" solve the puzzle? Are you absolutely sure? Or is it more accurate to say that "I have not yet solved it?"

The danger of "can't" is that it is a setup for failure. If I believe I can, or I cannot do something, I'll be right because I will give up.

But

But is a common word that connects two thoughts. The issue is that it negates the first half of the sentence. Imagine if a loved one tells you, "I love you, but..." You immediately negate the "I love you" and focus on the negative that follows.

Consider replacing "but" with "and." For example, "I love you, and I feel frustrated when you are late [Therefore, I request that you could help me by being on time]."

Try

Try is unclear, lacks commitment, and is often inaccurate. When I ask my wife to pick up the dry-cleaning, and the response is "I'll try," I do not know if I can count on it or if I should get the dry cleaning myself. It would be clearer to directly reply, "Yes, I will," or "No, I won't." I could also offer a counteroffer such as, "I am busy today, so I am not sure if I will have enough time to do so. Can I call you to let you know later this afternoon?"

To explore "try," take a moment to place a pencil on the floor. Now "try" to pick it up. You will quickly find that there is no such thing as "try." You either pick up the pencil, or you do not.

Hard /Difficult

These words are whiny and disempowering. If I tell you that "I am assigning a task and it is really hard," how does it feel? Threatening, frustrating, and generally sets me up for a focus on the stress of the task. Imagine instead that I tell you that "I am assigning a task and it will be a bit of a challenge. Are you up for the challenge?" Notice how this may bring a bit of nervousness and can feel more energizing/engaging.

When I use these words, it tends to be an excuse not to act. What if the task is not truly "difficult" but rather difficult *for me*? Consider is it "difficult" to shoot a basket in basketball? For me, perhaps yes. For Michael Jordan, perhaps no. What is the key difference between us? Practice.

I could become better at any task with enough practice. Another option to replace "difficult" is either "I am a beginner" or "I am practicing." This subtle shift brings the focus away from the limitations and toward the possibilities.

Problem

This word immediately creates suffering about the situation. Perhaps most famously is the line, "Houston we have a problem," associated with the trouble experienced by the Apollo 13 space shuttle. Notice how this statement immediately focuses us on the problem rather than the problem-solving. A very simple replacement is to reframe as "The situation is X. What are the possibilities or solutions?" Notice how quickly this reduces fear and focuses on solving the concern.

CHAPTER 20

EMOTIONS AND RELATIONSHIPS
⟍⟍⟍⟍⟍ ⟋⟋⟋⟋⟋

Love is a combination of admiration, respect, and passion.
If you have one of those going, that's par for the course.
If you have two, you aren't quite world class but you're close.
If you have all three, then you don't need to die;
you're already in Heaven.
- William Wharton

The best feeling in the world is...
When you look at that special person and
they are already smiling at you.
- Anonymous

Much of this book has focused on my personal emotions. However, my feelings exist in a larger context, as well. We have a range of relationships in our lives that balance our emotional responses. If we attempt to change, these relationships will guide us back to where we were. In order to successfully change myself, I must also consider the impact on those around me. For this chapter, we will be focusing primarily on our primary romantic relationships, but many of the principles will apply to all of our relationships.

Developing Relationships

Relationships often develop through stages. Initially, we may have a time where we "put our best foot forward." This stage often involves hiding certain things which we consider to be vulnerable, inappropriate, or could lead to judgment. At this point, individuals maintain a certain superficiality as the relationship is established.

As a relationship becomes established, we develop trust over time. We learn how our emotions, goals, and desires interact with each other and begin to share our differences.

Over time and commitment, we develop knowledge not only of each other's superficial image but also of each other's limits with the trust that comes with being able to be ourselves. We can know that it is OK to have differences of opinion and different interests.

It is said that dolphins are an animal species that pair-bond. When they do so, one can observe the two dolphins playing and swimming together. At other times, they play and swim apart before returning together again. Just the same in human relationships, there may be times when we are together or apart, but still connected by the bonds of the relationship.

At times, relationships can become toxic, with accumulated guilt and anger. For example, illness, infidelity, or abuse can make these relationships uncomfortable or unsafe, leading to a separation.

Deepening Trust

How do we deepen trust to move forward in relationships? There are two ways to deepen trust, by accident and by choice. Commonly, trust develops by accident. As we spend time together, trust slowly builds along with our familiarity.

Trust is also a choice. Trust is a gift we choose to give to someone. Consider a secret you have held for some time. You may be able to remember the moment of anxiety sharing that secret with someone. Like jumping into a pool in the summertime, there is a moment of decision and a leap of faith. This is a moment of choosing trust, hoping that the other will be ready to catch us.

We can practice giving trust in a range of ways. By sharing our self-judgments, we build trust over time. There is also the added benefit that if we expose our beliefs to light, we may discover they were not as real as we feared or that they are easier to bear as a shared burden.

To practice:

- Share one thing that scares you
- Share one way you judge yourself
- Share one feeling of being unsuccessful
- Share one moment of feeling uneasy, unbalanced, or weak.
- Share one feeling of shame
- Practice honesty and consistency

Giving and Receiving

In relationships, I need to consider not only my own ability to balance each of the five key emotions but also how my experience interacts with my beloved. Just like my emotions ebb and flow over time, in the context of a relationship, there will be changes in the balance of emotions. The intent is to move toward some level of balanced and symmetrical give-and-take across these different emotional areas.

Courage

Relationships require courage, to express ourselves, and to listen to the other. Sometimes, situations require some dialogue and brainstorming before jumping to a single solution. This process of brainstorming, listening, and working together can strengthen a relationship. In contrast, fear can leave us isolated.

Vision

Do I know what I want and where I am headed? Can I assertively communicate these goals with my partner and negotiate differences? Effective drive and communication can grow a partnership together. In contrast, passivity can lead to shame or anger.

Joy

When good things happen, we can share successes as well as challenges. This partnership helps us to reinforce our success and lessen the weight of challenges. In contrast, isolation can lead to boredom and loneliness.

Compassion

Bruises happen. Can we support each other as bruises happen over the course of time? At different times, I may be the "strong one" wiping away tears, and at other times I may surrender to the support from my beloved. In contrast, a lack of support can lead to fear.

Respect

Honoring each other helps to strengthen a relationship. We love and respect each other, warts and all. This does not mean we do not work on improving ourselves, but it is within a larger context of sharing our wounds in a larger circle of trust and safety.

Love

While we may love many people, there is a special level of love between partners. This larger circle creates the safety to hold the range of emotions and to be able to explore together.

Examining My Relationship

Consider your personal relationship and ask yourself:

- Am I able to give courage, drive, joy, compassion, and respect?
    - o If not, how can I practice the skill to do so?

- Am I willing to give courage, drive, joy, compassion, and respect?
    - o If not, how can I develop the trust to do so?

- Do I actively give courage, drive, joy, compassion, and respect?
    - o If not, how can I build awareness?

- Does my partner offer me courage, drive, joy, compassion, and respect?
    - o If not, can I ask for help?

- When my partner offers, do I allow myself to receive courage, drive, joy, compassion, and respect?
    - o If not, what can I let go of to allow myself to be able to receive the love they offer me?

- Is each of these feelings balanced over time, with each of us giving and receiving?
    - o If not, what can I give to help bring balance?

Our intimate relationship is a workshop where we have the opportunity to grow ourselves, together. Even if an attempt has not worked in the past, continue to explore how you can approach it differently, to find success. When I am ready to heal and change, I bring my partner along with me.

CHAPTER 21

EMOTIONS AND
THE WORKPLACE
❥❥❥❥❥❥ ❥❥❥❥❥

The culture of a workplace - an organization's
values, norms, and practices - has a huge impact on
our happiness and success.
- Adam Grant

Our workplace is a place of business. Some think that there is no place for emotion in this setting. However, as we have discussed, emotions are a part of all we do. We are not machines, even if we do not express them in the same manner.

As individuals, when our emotions are out of balance, we feel "dis-ease." As an organization, when we do not attend to the emotional culture of the organization, there will also be "dis-ease" which may take the form of turnover, reduced productivity, lost revenue, workers compensation claims, accidents, and a whole range of other negative possibilities. These elements are the health measures of the organization, but they are rooted in the health of the organizational culture.

While we do not "do therapy" at work, therapy is about maintaining our highest levels of effective functioning, free from issues that get in the way. This may include effective development, planning/goal setting, achieving key metrics, long-term stability, and revenue. This may vary across an organization, as well as within a single division or unit within a larger organization.

Ask myself:

- Do I listen to my employees/co-workers?
- Do they feel "heard" by me?
- Am I able to "brainstorm" new and creative solutions for consideration?
- Can I articulate a clear vision and mission for our organization and our department?
- Do I clearly understand my specific role in achieving that mission?
- Are the key metrics of success achievable?
- Am I able to achieve "success" on a daily basis?
- Am I able to smile at least once on a daily basis (not including when it's time to go home)?
- Am I able to laugh while at work?
- Do I feel *a part of* my team, or *apart from* my team?
- Do we celebrate shared successes, birthdays, or other events?
- Am I able to collaborate on projects?
- Am I able to mentor others in some way?
- Do we support each other in our tasks?
- Do I feel respected and valued for my skills?
- Do I feel respected and valued as an individual?
- Do we say, "Thank you," "Good Job," or other acknowledgments?

- Do we use structure and systems to maintain stability and effective functioning?

If I answered "no" to any of these, what small steps can I take today to bring a change?

Emotions

Fear/Courage

Fear kills creativity and can "freeze" productivity. There are many things to be fearful of at work, such as:

- The boss's disapproval
- Disciplinary action
- Being fired
- Sexual harassment
- Overt or subtle harassment is based on my gender, race, religion, or other personal characteristics.
- Fear of failure
- Fear of making mistakes
- Fear of success
- Fear of not knowing what to do

In contrast, with courage, individuals are confident to identify possibilities, propose solutions, and complete tasks fluidly.

Assertiveness

Anger and aggressiveness are toxic in an organization. Anger often ties closely to fear, with fear being at the root of anger and anger causing more fear. Similarly, aggression can cause passive stagnation.

Within healthy functioning organizations, there is a free flow of communication in every direction. This includes ideas, suggestions, requests, and supportive coaching.

Passion

When the team believes strongly in the mission, we can accomplish anything. We are indeed stronger together when we can find common goals and share our strengths to achieve them. If we are in competition for ourselves, we run the risk of damaging other people's success rather than supporting the team. In business, another risk is that when individuals become overworked, they can fatigue and make costly mistakes. It is important to balance the passion for playing hard with times of rest, such as lunch breaks and vacations. With stress, there is a progressive increase in activity, but if it is too much, we face a sharp decline in productivity.

Within healthy organizations, there are shared goals, activities, passions, and successes. Finding some pleasure and fun in work can strengthen our ability to be effective and productive.

Compassion

Indifference creates isolation and resentment. Without a supportive team and mentorship, individuals can feel alone. Unable to trust the organization, our motivation can diminish, and we can seek to leave. Meanwhile, productivity diminishes, the staff left behind becomes stressed, and each new employee requires time to learn the new position. Rapid change can be destabilizing to relationships and the stable structure needed for operations.

In healthy organizations, there are supportive relationships. There is an ability to ask for help and a commitment to supporting, mentoring, promoting, and otherwise growing ourselves and our team. There is a feeling of trust in the stability of the organization; each employee feels secure that it's *my* job and *my* relationships. Safety is a core human need. Having it allows us to focus on higher goals like work tasks. When emergency situations occur requiring rapid change, consider methods to quickly restore stability when the crisis has passed.

Respect

Lack of respect is dangerous in the workplace. This can lead to a wide range of harms, from verbal jabs to covert sabotage and even overt harassment. Respect does not mean that we agree on everything, but we respect each other for our similarities as well as our differences.

In healthy organizations, there is a respect for the individual, the team, the process, and the mission. There are structure and systems to help guide and manage, improving consistency and stability. As we understand the value in ourselves and those around us, it is easier to focus on the mission of success.

Tools

Semi-Annual Retreat

Bring staff together to take stock on what is functioning well and what things can be changed. Including team-building exercises can create a collaborative environment and foster supportive relationships. Positive relationships are the invisible glue that supports organizational functioning

Do as I Do

We are all a part of the organization. At every moment, we are role models. Are we demonstrating effective behaviors or role modeling damaging communication? Just for today, we can strive to be a positive role model, with our actions matching our words.

Awards

There are many ways to reward desired behaviors. Certificates, plaques, applause, a desirable parking space, can all be used both as incentives and acknowledgment of good behaviors. These can be specific, such as achieving perfect attendance, showing you are a team player, or "the most improved" in a key performance metric. These public acknowledgments not only support the individual's success, but also can improve the morale and motivation of others, who see that efforts are recognized.

Regular Communication

There are many tools for communication that can be used to solicit input, maintain consistency, and create a vision for the future. Communication is not a "once and done" event. Consider multiple tools and venues to promote communication of a range of information, including both success and areas of growth. Different procedures can be used to share information with my supervisees, my department, internal organization, and external communications. Remember that real communication is "two-way."

Honest Communication

Honesty can be scary, but it often communicates the most important pieces of information. Having multiple methods of 360-degree communication can help to prevent problem development and maintain functions. Consider also anonymous options for those who do not feel safe in communications. Consider tools to establish trust and honesty in communication to be understood as a valued support, rather than a threat.

The Attitude of "Trial and Error" Learning

Knowing that we never stop learning and growing, we will continue to have new activities. It is important to maintain a "safe space" where mistakes are understood as part of the growth process. From this context, "problems" are requests for help as we grow. When individuals are afraid to make mistakes, there can be challenges since it is impossible to have a pre-trained policy and procedure for every situation. Progressive discipline is an increase in structure and support as we build our skills, rather than a punishment. While there may be a few areas that require an employee to terminate the relationship, these are clear and severe. In contrast, the majority of failures can be managed through education, coaching, and support.

Collaborative Practice

When implementing a new practice, it is important to gain support. By inviting suggestions and collaborative development of the procedures, we can create more employee "buy-in" and willingness to implement the new task. Further, collaborative efforts have been found to have more productive and effective results since the valuable and diverse experience of the team can identify risk areas as well as improvement opportunities.

Prioritization

We all have many tasks. It is important to know which one is our priority so that it can maintain the most effort. Remember also that urgent and unexpected situations will always arise. Consider having "emergency management" as one of our priorities. Consider having "structure maintenance" as another, since it prevents emergencies.

Beliefs

What is the unconscious (or conscious) beliefs that I hold about business operations? For example:

- I know how to be successful, if only people would listen to me.
- I hate my workplace.
- My office is so "messed up."
- Staff/coworkers should follow directions and do what they are told.
- Staff/coworkers should do their darned job.
- Staff/coworkers are lazy.
- Staff/coworkers are out to get me/sabotage me.
- My boss hates me.
- My boss will "get me" if I make a mistake.
- Our office works better as a team.
- Our office works better if I have a plan and they follow it.
- Our office works better, following my vision.
- Our office works better when the team buys into the vision.
- If only [insert challenge here] was resolved, then work would be great.

Consider also:

- Where did I get some of these beliefs about the workplace?
- Are there other beliefs that would better serve me at work?

- Can I set a date when I will let go of the old beliefs and adopt the new beliefs?

Notice how our internal beliefs can change my relationships in the workplace. These beliefs can change the way the workplace functions.

Practice

There are many ways to practice in the workplace as we increase awareness and skill with emotional balance. These tools can vary depending upon which specific area is needed. For example:

- Start a "suggestion box."

- Have a conversation with an "opponent," maintaining the intent of listening, rather than judging what they have to say

- Ask individuals to individually brainstorm solutions to share before deciding on a course of action

- Review all or part of the mission statement at a staff meeting

- Discuss my personal role in the mission during a staff meeting

- Review a policy procedure in a staff meeting

- Plan steps for a given challenge or need

- Plan for my individual growth through mentoring, training, or other means needed for promotion or skill enhancements

- Include group activities with shared efforts

- Celebrate a success

- Offer to support a colleague on one task today

- Ask a colleague for help on one task today

- Thank someone today

CHAPTER 22

EMOTIONS AND ADDICTION

Our greatest glory is not in never falling,
but in getting up every time we do.
- Confucius

How Does Addiction Develop Over Time?

Addiction involves a process of repeated behaviors that cause the need for more (tolerance) and discomfort if one continues (withdrawal). This does not happen with one event, but over time. For this discussion, we will consider the process of addiction, which can include both substance use, as well as process addictions such as gambling or other behaviors.

Example of 2 Brain Pathways

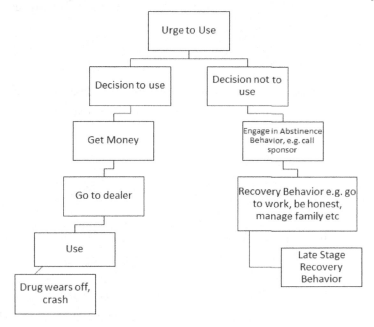

Let's continue the discussion of how the brain works, with an example as it relates to substance use. In the image above, imagine that each box is a brain cell that connects to the next brain cell. This is a simplification since each cell actually connects to many more cells. Bob has a thought or urges to use a drug. He decides to use it, so he goes to get money (perhaps through his preferred illegal means), goes to his dealer to obtain the substance, uses it until it is all gone, and finally, the drug wears off, and he crashes. This, of course, can create a cycle where Bob has the urge to use again, and the process repeats.

He repeats this cycle today, and tonight, then tomorrow, and again the following day. It repeats again and again and again over the course of addiction for ten years. It is like the rain cloud that causes water to pool into a creek. Over time, the creek gets carved out deeper into a river bed, then eventually it becomes the Mississippi River, and eventually, the Grand Canyon.

Disease Model

This is a simple way of understanding the disease model of addiction. The disease model says that substance use disorder is:

1) Potentially fatal
2) Progressive
3) Chronic
4) Treatable

This is just like other chronic conditions such as diabetes, heart disease, and obesity, which achieve similar recovery rates.

> *Potentially fatal:* We know that each of these behavioral patterns is potentially fatal, through heart attacks, drug overdoses, and risk to the cardiovascular system.

> *Progressive:* Just like the Grand Canyon example, substance use disorder is progressive. One begins to drink or use drugs more and more, while the habitual pathway becomes stronger and stronger.

> *Chronic:* Substance use disorder is also chronic. Just like learning our times tables, once a Grand Canyon has developed, there is no substantive approach to removing it. This can explain why individuals who relapse start substance use at the same level as they used previously at the level of depth of the learned behavior(s).

Treatable: Today, an estimated 24 million Americans are in recovery from substance use disorder. With proper treatment, long-term recovery is the expected outcome. Just like with pneumonia, treatment is typically successful when it is long enough and strong enough.

Decisions and the Free Will Conundrum

In this example, it appears that it all starts with that one bad decision. So, doesn't that mean that this is all a choice, and they could just stop any time they want? Yes and no.

Autopilot: When we are on autopilot, sleepwalking through life, we are not making choices. Although, strictly speaking, we are able to make choices, we often are not doing so. Most of our potential choices are on autopilot since there are too many decisions happening simultaneously to track them all purposely.

Inertia: The law of inertia says that once an object is in motion, it tends to stay in motion unless acted on by an outside force. When we have an ingrained pattern, like a strong river current, it pulls us along, even if we were to decide to change. Similarly, once I go to the amusement park and strap into the roller coaster, even if I change my mind, I am going along for the ride. From this point, how can I possibly get out? There is only one way, intervention by an external force. For example, the power goes out, and the operator engages the emergency brake. In the case of a substance use disorder, the cycle tends to continue until some outside force can contain me. Often this is pressure from the criminal justice system, child welfare, or perhaps my employer or spouse.

Free Will: So, when do we have free will? When we hit the "pause" button, and metaphorically stand up and look around at the playing field. For this brief moment, we can choose another direction or choose to continue on the old, well-worn path. Free will happens in very brief moments of awareness. This is just the same as relapse. When I work with someone who had years of sobriety before a "sudden" relapse, I can usually trace a gradual escalation of mild risk behaviors back about six months (for example, stopping going to meetings, withdrawing from peers, feeling depressed). This may be largely on autopilot. However, there is typically a precise moment in time that can be recalled and pinpointed, for example, at a 5 P.M. on Friday. At this moment, one can recall the feeling of stress and the split-second decision to "forget this" and seek to use a substance. How many of our life changes are made in this way?

Example of 2 Brain Pathways

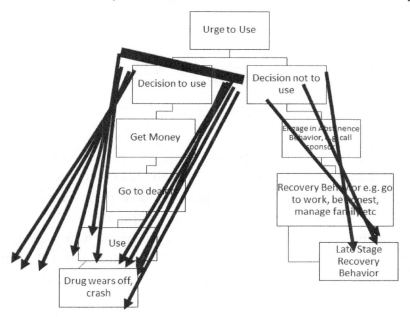

Treatment and Recovery

We have examined the development of an addiction process. Now we turn to recovery. As with this image of the brain, we have an imaginary Grand Canyon of ten years of practice on the addiction pathway and an imaginary trickle of water on the recovery pathway. So, the helicopter comes in and saves me from the rushing waters.

Now what? I go to a treatment program, and they give me five days of medical stabilization before the funder declares me "cured" and able to be managed with a less intensive form of treatment. Does the recovery (right-hand) pathway appear to be ready to handle this yet? If it took ten years to build the Grand Canyon on the addiction pathway, how long would it take to build a similar pathway on the

171

recovery path? (This is not a trick question) The answer would reasonably be, about ten years, or at least a lot longer than funders pay for treatment these days. However, each day of those ten years is substance-free, building practice in recovery, so it becomes easier and more fulfilling over time.

So How Does One Become Well?

Step 1: Going to Treatment

While a very few people do spontaneously go on their own, it is most common that people do not go until the helicopter comes to pull them out of the river. In the beginning, most all motivation is externally based. Consider that in national data, only around ten percent of those in need of treatment actually access it in a given year. So those agreeing (or being told) to go to treatment will, by their nature, be a bit more severe in their Grand Canyon development.

Note that treatment in this context is referring to licensed substance use disorder treatment. There are many pathways to recovery, and many supports that may be part of this journey.

Step 2: Build a Wall

Create some barriers to the old pathway for some initial stability by working with a licensed drug and alcohol professional in your state. Building a wall may include a range of supports to quickly change triggering associations and increase supports while one has time to establish and strengthen a recovery pathway. This is particularly important at the beginning when the old pathway is very strong and the new pathway is weak.

This decision to build a wall is not taken lightly and should not be done alone, but with the support of a licensed substance use disorder professional in your area. They will help with a complete assessment to help determine what intensity of substance use disorder and what form of addiction treatment is needed. Professionals can also help you choose which supportive options may be best for you, such as medications, housing, case management, peer support, or something else. Peer support is an important component since there is often easy access and supports are free of charge. Remember that these other supportive options are not treatment, as described here, but rather support to fill gaps in a complex set of needs.

In an outpatient treatment setting, this critical step can be very challenging, since it is an internal strength of will to refrain from the addictive behaviors in the days between treatment sessions. This internal strength of will is quite difficult considering that the definition of the disorder is that one is not able to control the substance use or other behavior.

For many people, this means going to jail, which is a sad way in which our country often starts the treatment process. Jail may begin abstinence due to the controlled environment, but without other services does nothing to address the complex needs discussed throughout this book, which are the core of long-term change and success.

For others, building a wall is achieved in a residential treatment program. The National Institute for Health reports that principles for effective treatment begin with a *minimum* of ninety days of residential substance use disorder treatment program (or outpatient treatment, if there was a lower initial severity) with limited effectiveness for programs less than ninety days and greater improvements for those who receive six to nine months. They note the best-known form of residential treatment is the therapeutic community, a specially structured environment focused on relationship building, emotional skills training, contingency management, and cognitive change. This evidence-based approach integrates some of the best elements of other approaches.

Based on the brain example, it is easy to understand why time is the best predictor of outcome. Similarly, it is easy to see why research finds that undertreatment brings with it a serious risk of relapse. The longer-term treatment actually is more cost-effective since it reduces relapse and the associated human and economic costs.

Step 3: Believe in a life more than I have lived

I remember working with an individual in prison. One day he asked, "What do you want me to do? Work at McDonald's?" Underneath this question was a deep belief that he was unable to do anything other than selling drugs and a life of crime. Once someone comes to treatment, they can be housed and somewhat sheltered from their active addiction process as the body begins to detoxify from years of substances and negative beliefs. It is only then that the treatment process begins. The core of this relationship is the trust in the counselor and the process, which takes time to develop. I have worked with individuals for six months, building trust before they reveal some of their secrets, some of which they have never admitted even to themselves, for example:

- "I was raped as a boy."
- "I hate myself."

- "Mom told me that I was a piece of trash, and I still believe that."

- "I am not strong enough to succeed."

Just as the Supreme Court determined, the counseling relationship is less like a relationship with a physician and more like one with a priest, rabbi, or clergy. Ask yourself, are there things you have never told anyone or had the courage to speak out loud? Would you tell them to someone in the first meeting? Consider also, to whom have you shared your most vulnerable secrets? What was it about those relationships that made it possible?

Once that trust is developed, then the deeper work beings. This is when we begin to unpack the roots of our addiction, from the past, from the present, from the fear of the future, and from our present-day beliefs. If I believe I am not able or unworthy, I will never progress. The therapy relationship and relationships with those in long term recovery give hope that there is life outside of what I used to believe was the limit of my existence.

At this stage, as we deal with traumas, it is important to have sensitivity. One needs to first build enough strength, or facing such demons can trigger a relapse or transition to a cross-addiction (e.g., Changing to gambling disorder or other addictive behavioral patterns). During this time, one also learns the skills to address these beliefs and the trusting relationships he or she can hold hands with, so that they are not alone. Only then can one feel the inner strength to stand up to these fading beliefs.

Step 4: Build a life worth living

Once we believe that more is possible, we can begin to do the work of establishing those changes and find what we want this new life to look like. How do we want relationships to flow? What type of vocation is right for me as a parent, a student, or an employee? What brings meaning to my life?

Step 5: Maintenance

Just like learning our times tables, or exercising at the gym, this brain pathway becomes strengthened over time. Once we get set on the right path, we practice, practice, practice until this becomes the new Grand Canyon.

Within recovery, there is increased trust in myself, a deeper sense of relationships with others, an ability to ask for help when needed, and the strength to share my heart when others are needed. The range of emotions that were drowned out by the addiction process is now free. Many of the emotions from my active addiction state are resolved so that I can be free of them, rather than controlled by them.

We considered that it might take ten years to build this new Grander Canyon. But life starts now. Even if I am in early recovery, today, I can visit dozens of states and countries. There are so many wonderful things to do. I don't even miss going to Arizona as I build my new Grander Canyon.

The therapy journey is unique for each individual, but it takes time, perseverance, trust, and safe relationships. We know that those who make it three days are more likely to make it a week. Those who make it a week are more likely to make it a month, and so on, with more and more time. ...And those who make it to five years, just like cancer, are considered to be unlikely to relapse again.

Ask yourself, if it were my brother or mother or child, would I want them to have only Step 1, or Step 1 through 5 and beyond? Perhaps our system should be geared in this direction, toward *lifelong* recovery, rather than acute-stage management.

Feelings Management in the Therapeutic Community

Within the therapeutic community tradition, there is a process called the feelings management group. Years ago, this had been called the encounter group, where individuals encounter each other in the honest sharing of emotion. This group process has been known as central to the success of treatment. Today, this structured process is designed specifically to communicate and process emotions.

This process occurs in the therapeutic community, a residential substance use disorder treatment program where individuals build relationships as they examine their personal beliefs, fears, and concerns together. This group is run by staff with training on how to manage this process safely, knowing where it is headed to help guide the discussion to resolution.

To engage in this process, one person identifies that they have an issue with another resident and notify staff so that they can be called on in the group. During the session, the person experiencing the feeling identifies:

1) What happened, specifically, what they saw or heard
2) What they feel or felt, and
3) What they want or need from the other person.

The other resident involved is guided to respond to each of the three steps, acknowledging the event, acknowledging the emotion, and responding to the request for resolution.

For example:

- Jane: Yesterday in the cafeteria, you stepped on my foot and kept on walking away. It hurt. I was really mad and felt like I didn't matter. I want you to pay attention to where you are walking and not do it anymore.

- Mary: I did walk by you yesterday. I didn't realize I stepped on your foot, but I am sorry. I didn't mean to hurt you. I do sometimes get distracted when I am chatting with my friends, but I am willing to try to pay closer attention, so it doesn't happen again.

This example shows how this process helps the person move through identification, create clear articulation, and complete the process and resolve a solution.

Often individuals will not speak their emotions, leading them to remain as they are. Sometimes, I am ready to speak but do not know exactly what was wrong, so it is hard to communicate. Sometimes I feel hurt or angry but don't know what I need to fix it.

This process may not run as smoothly as the example above but knowing the roadmap to where you are going increases the chances of success. Doing so builds authentic relationships, develops trust, and establishes skills to manage emotions rather than "stuffing" them or having them come out "sideways" in some other harmful way such as revenge or continued substance use.

Long-term Recovery

What does long term recovery look like?

- Does it mean continuing to be disabled and unable to work?

- Does it mean standing in a long line daily to get my dose of opioid replacement medication?

- Does it mean being unable to laugh and have fun with friends?

- Does it mean not being able to parent my children safely?

These are difficult questions. Most research looks only at things in weeks or months. Recovery begins early but is measured in years. The things that were helpful for day one of the journey are very different than day 30, or day 365, or day 1,825 (five years).

It is important to study those who made it to five years to learn what has long-term gain rather than short-term cost savings. Said another way, providing three days of antibiotic provides successful cost savings and symptom remission, but is poor for long-term cost savings and success because of the expected relapse.

Recovery is a process, an active movement in the direction of a progressively healthier and fuller life. While relapse can happen, the longer one maintains in recovery, the more an individual wants more and knows that they are capable of more.

Faces and Voices of Recovery did a survey to consider what recovery looks like. Among 3,000 individuals in recovery for an average of ten years, they found dramatic changes and growth reflective of citizenry, success, and proactive health promotion. Said another way, people in stable recovery are considered to be "better than well" since they have often developed awareness, personal responsibility, and emotional maturity beyond many in the general public (which of course has about ninety percent of those with active substance use disorder, since most do not seek treatment).

What do we want for our brothers and sisters struggling with addiction? Is it just to stop lying and breaking into cars? Or is it a larger goal to find peace and fulfill who they were meant to be before substances created a detour?

How do we remember the potential they held at age six, long before most have ever used any substance?

How do we help them to deeply know that this not only possible, but that long-term recovery is our expectation?

How can we learn from some of these individuals who have had the courage to complete a fearless moral inventory, face their most challenging emotions, and achieve mastery and success of this critical skill, to find balance in the range of emotions, and joy of living that comes from this balance?

This is the work of treatment and the promise of recovery.

Emotions of Recovery

With addiction processes, it is easy to get caught up in the behaviors, such as lying to get money, the behaviors of using substances, the behaviors that damage relationships, the behaviors which are perhaps illegal. During the addiction process, there is often a roller-coaster mix of emotions as well, ranging from fear of being found out, fear of lack, fear of withdrawal, anger at being embarrassed, or shame over the behaviors.

When you talk to people about recovery, there are a few emotional themes that emerge: Drive, gratitude, and connection. Understanding the experience of recovery can help to give the courage to persevere through to the next steps.

Courage

Achieving recovery requires a deep personal awareness and courage to face the fears and shame that have held us stuck in addiction. Guilt can seem so big that it is overwhelming. The recovery journey includes the courage to face life on life's terms and to rise above our personal shame. Imagine having this as a skill. This is the courage we need for our work, our relationships, and to take many health risks to achieve a more successful and fulfilling life.

Drive

Recovery is a verb. It is an active state of growth. It is having achieved the recovery required a sustained effort to withstand urges and maintain inertia in a positive direction to reduce the risk of sliding back into a relapse. It is like getting on the space shuttle to blast off, away from the pull of gravity. Having practiced this drive, this has become a strength. Many of those I know in long-term recovery are the strongest, most driven individuals I know. This is not by accident. Without this drive, they would not have been able to pull away from the intense gravitational pull of the disease of addiction.

Connection

In speaking to those in recovery, there is often a theme of a deep connection that is difficult to describe. Imagine for a moment sitting with your deepest shame that you feel is so bad that it could never be spoken. Then sharing that with the group that you are working with, be that a peer support group or professional therapy group. Doing so takes a deep trust in the group to take the risk and understanding of the meeting as a safe space.

When we give this level of trust to others, there is a deep sense of connection, the root of love. It is said that our success is measured by how far we have come. The addiction process is a disease of isolation. The recovery process includes a sharp shift to the depth of connections.

These are honest relationships rather than superficial ones. This may be one of the most authentic relationships where we feel the safety to "confess" our weaknesses and grow beyond them. These are the people we long to see in our lives and feel sad when they go away. While we cannot have all of our relationships in this manner, particularly the peer support system of addiction recovery is a deep and ongoing practice of this relationship skill.

Compassionate Giving

The addiction process activates the fight or flight danger portion of the brain. This chronic emergency status of running away from withdrawal leads to an intense focus on myself, perceived as selfishness.

As I move toward recovery, there is a process of cleaning up the damage we have made in our relationships. Many individuals continue this further into recovery. The 12th step of the 12-step tradition is about giving back. Many times, we live with a sense of scarcity or lack in the addiction cycle.

This recovery process is centered on a feeling of abundance; that I have come so far that I am able to give. That so much has been given to me; it is my duty to give back. This is another example of how those in recovery can be better than well. In America, only about half our country goes to vote. In contrast, long-term recovery includes awareness of my civic duties, with a voting rate of over eighty-five percent in those surveyed. Imagine a world where giving and supporting one another is a reality, and a norm.

Gratitude

The addiction process is marked by deep shame and feelings of unworthiness. I may not believe I can be better, but even if I could, I don't believe I deserve it.

Recovery requires one to rise above these beliefs, to reclaim our inner value. To act today in ways that are reflective of that innate work, and to continue to be this positive role model for others. Gratitude is an attitude that helps to achieve and maintain this skill. I am grateful for the things that I value. I am grateful for the value that I have become aware of.

This is often part of the journey, to practice gratitude. For example, start a journal with three things each day you are grateful for. By practicing gratitude, the preciousness of life is remembered. By practicing daily, over time, we suddenly have an entire book to remind us of our worth, and the worth of the life around us. What a precious gift this is, one that so many people long for.

For Those with Loved ones Struggling with Addiction

If we are helping a loved one through their process, it is important for us to understand the dark feelings in addiction, the path of change, and the vision of recovery. This helps us to maintain hope. It helps us to avoid distractions to the recovery journey. It helps us to remember even on the days when they cannot yet see a vision of recovery. It helps us to be as effective as possible, in recovering our loved ones.

CHAPTER 23

EMOTIONS AND CULTURE
❰❰❰❰❰❰ ❱❱❱❱❱

A nation's culture resides in the hearts
and in the soul of its people.
- Mahatma Gandhi

Our Experience of Culture

The experience of emotions from a cultural perspective varies based on a person's world view. As an example, Euro-American cultures tend to have views based on the value of independence (e.g., Being the best that I can) while African and Asian cultures may emphasize interdependence (e.g., Understanding how my actions are deeply connected with my family bringing shame or honor).

These basic world views can lead to differences in values such as competition versus cooperation, or individual rights versus collective responsibility. This can also lead to differences in ethical principles, such as feeling control over nature versus being "one with nature," or survival of the fittest versus survival of the tribe.

The experience of emotions, as well as their response to treatment approaches, vary dramatically across countries around the world.

Race, gender, culture, and other social constructs (i.e., environmental experiences, socioeconomic status) can create deep patterns in how to manage emotions. It is important to listen to an individual's story and their relationships while understanding how the story is filtered through their culture.

At the same time, it is important to remember that while cultural differences are extremely important, there are individual differences within each and every culture, based on the level of acculturation of the personal and community culture (for example, Americans who have been in the USA for four generations see things differently than those who are first-generation and not assimilated into the dominant culture). So, we watch for both cultural themes and each person's valuable individual story and experience

This basic sense of "who I am" affects 1) my internal thoughts, beliefs, and perceptions, 2) how I feel emotionally, and 3) how I relate to others around me.

Cultural Filters

Recalling our previous discussion on how my life experiences affect my mental filters and emotional reactions, let's consider how this applies in terms of culture.

Imagine a person growing up in a family of the same race, culture, and religion as you. In our formative years, we are trained in the culture of our families. We may learn the family holiday traditions, we are given clothes and toys for "boys" or "girls," we observe our family religious practices, or not, and we learn messages about others who look the same as we do, or not.

As we mature and start school, these patterns are reinforced by our peer group, which may conflict or reinforce the experience at home. Perhaps we will be rewarded for compliance or teased and bullied for non-compliance. As we mature into adulthood, we see images on television and politics with messages that reinforce these beliefs. As adults, we perhaps live in neighborhoods with other people who look or believe like us.

This becomes so common that we have blinders to it since it is simply "normal." In reality, these are like a telescopic lens we put on in childhood. These filters subtly narrow our personal experience of "reality." Instead of the truth, we can see only our filters of what it means to be a man/woman, rich/poor, Christian/Muslim, gay/straight, White/Black, and all the variations in these categories.

As new experiences occur to us, we file them, not based on reality, but based on these filters, accentuating our belief that the filters are real. Understand that this does not trivialize one's individual experience of reality, but rather informs the depths of the importance of collective cultural experience and how our personal beliefs are connected with the experiences of others around us.

We all experience these filters in one way or another. I can recall a time years ago during a long meeting when I suddenly looked around and realized I was the only white male in the room. What did this mean? This is not a situation I am typically in. What is it like for those in this situation consistently? This helped give me an awareness of what it might be like for other populations. As we discussed above, awareness heals. Our blindness can perpetuate existing challenges. This can take time but is a worthy effort to raise understanding.

These factors influence our relationships and interactions. Within 10-to-20 seconds of meeting someone, we have typically identified similar external characteristics and formed judgments about the individual. We make these judgments, with all of our life experience and mental associations with persons of that characteristic such as gender. However, this means we bring filters before we even say "hello" that can shape the conversation and relationship.

Now take a moment to consider an alternate scenario with just one difference from the example above. Imagine you are growing up in a family that is different from you in many characteristics, such as a different gender, race, or political ideation. What is it like being "different" on a daily basis, through holidays, through schools, through communities, through TV shows over the course of years? Consider also the challenges of having a different race (which is visible externally) as compared with having a different religion or sexual orientation (which may not be visible externally). This could create very different filters that we can only begin to understand. Now take a moment to consider the person on the other side of my expectations/judgments. How does my judgment raise reactive responses in them?

Raising Cultural Awareness

If I am unaware of how my filters are prejudicial, how do I break free of that denial? Awareness...

Raising our cultural awareness is the first step toward developing cultural competence. We all have areas where we are members of a dominant culture as well as a "minority" culture (remember that minority is not simply the number of individuals. Women have a larger number of individuals although they experience minority status).

Consider the following: In which of these areas am I in a majority role in this country?

- Gender

- Sexual Orientation

- Religion

- Race

- Ethnicity

- Political Party

- National Heritage

- Physical Abilities

- Mental Abilities

- Educational Status

- Socioeconomic Status

Based on these factors, I have a lived experience. For some individuals, we are in a majority role in some areas and in a minority role in others. While all of these categories are not equal, they can be a starting point for understanding.

If I am not sure whether I am in a majority role in one of these categories, then that may be a good place to start, raising awareness of how my experience connects to the world.

For any of the categories where you are *not in a majority* role, are you able to recall examples of difficulties you have experienced as a result of that status? What emotions did this cause in you? If it is very easy for us to find examples of this kind of experience, what does that tell us about our mental filters?

For any of the categories where you *are in the majority* role, are you able to recall examples of times when someone believed or accused you of causing them difficulty? What emotions did this cause in you?

If we have trouble identifying this kind of experience, what does that tell us about our personal mental filters?

Times of developing this awareness can bring the motivation to cause us to change.

To a greater or lesser degree, we all experience impacts from our "minority" status in one of these categories. If we have experienced a minimal impact, how does that shape our mental filters of this issue? Does that mean we do not recognize gender and racial differences? Does this lack of awareness put us at risk of discriminating behaviors that may be unintended but may reinforce perception and experience of harm when received by those of a "minority" status?

Remember also that "difference" does not mean "less than."

We may think of prejudice as an active hatred of another group, with active harmful intent. However, just like our discussion of communication styles, our pre-judgments range from passive impacts to aggressive impacts.

In areas where you are in the majority role, which emotions have arisen in your experience? Perhaps there is anger at an accusation of prejudice, fear of negative impacts including verbal and physical attacks, or hurt at feeling misunderstood. What is it like for someone to live with years of anger, fear, and hurt?

In areas where you are in the minority role, what are some of the emotions that have arisen? Perhaps there is loneliness at being alone, anger at being victimized, fear of harm or safety concerns, the heartache of being "invisible," or the hopelessness of believing it will never change. What is it like for someone to live with years of loneliness, anger, and fear? After prolonged isolation and experience of discrimination, is it surprising that this frustration could lead to a desire to be heard? There are regular protests for a wide range of these issues as people struggle to be heard and understood.

While sometimes stereotypes of a White man or a Black woman are true for an individual, we must be very careful that our filters do not blind us to the specific situation in front of us. There is a wide range of attitudes and experiences among people in any of these majority/minority categories. Understanding this, how do we move toward understanding "Joe the person," rather than having him "pegged" based on one of these characteristics that become stereotyped? We begin with an awareness of these differences. We can start this process with a book, but at some point, to understand, it is important to reach out to others of the minority/majority role to deepen our understanding.

Over the course of generations, these cultural differences can break down further, so that we relate to others based on our personal experience, rather than based on the experience of my ancestors. This can further be complicated when generations of a practiced emotional and relational pattern can create the experience of hopelessness or permanence, which requires time to change. For example, in the U.S., a women's right to vote took generations to achieve and culturally process.

Gender

Men and women see things differently based on their socialization. Virtually all of the mood disorders are twice as common in women as they are in men. Does this mean that women experience anxiety and depression twice as often as men? Maybe or maybe not.

Men and women are socialized differently in a variety of ways. For example, men can be more behaviorally expressive or angry, which can create challenges when they withhold other emotions, perhaps becoming abusive. Women, in contrast, are permitted to have a wider range of emotions, including "soft" emotions and actions such as tenderness and crying. This can lead to becoming victims or being labeled badly if they express anger.

When we step back, we can also see that men are twice as likely as women to experience virtually all of the behaviorally-based disorders such as addiction. In this light, it is curious to consider if men and women experience different rates of depression and sadness or if they express it differently based in part on this cultural socialization. For example, women more commonly used social supports as a coping mechanism, reflecting a willingness to share these emotions that are commonly understood. In contrast, many men have been shamed for their expression of emotions, so they may be more apt to engage in other activities to numb these feelings, such as the use of alcohol.

Understanding these differences, we may begin to work with women to develop tools to balance and expand the range of acceptable emotions. Examples of this could include things like journaling and cognitive therapy.

In contrast, for men, it is important to develop a safe space to increase awareness and experience of vulnerable emotions. At times, external activities can be used to mitigate the anxiety caused by the direct expression of emotion. Examples can include things like discussions that occur over meals, fishing, playing golf, or other similar activities that allow time together to discuss things calmly.

With gender, there can be a greater experience of violence, sexual assault, and other very serious impacts. There can also be subtle systemic discrimination, such as the difference in the average salary for a man and woman performing the same job. This type of discrimination may be difficult to prove in a specific case, but our lack of awareness of it can make us a part of the problem (allowing it to perpetuate) rather than part of a solution. Even though these harms may not be intentional, they can be damaging.

In addition to worldview, there are differences in linguistic and nonverbal communication patterns among men and women (and other cultural groups). For example, how far we stand from each other when speaking and norms about "turn-taking" or interrupting in conversations.

Race

Race is an area that has been emotionally charged for centuries. Wars have been fought over this issue. We have discussed how mental filters based on our experiences can shape our personal perceptions over the course of a lifetime. Consider culture further as it creates a deep communal filter for lived experiences:

- What happens when an entire race adopts a certain set of mental filters through their communal lived experiences?

- What happens when that race has experienced the same emotional, physical, and cultural experience for generations?

- What happens when another race experiences a different emotional, physical, and cultural experience, for generations?

We are expanding our awareness as a first step. It becomes clear that our mental beliefs and emotional wounds that we have practiced for years have been reinforced, not only by our personal experience but also reinforced by the collective history of my family, my neighborhood, and my racial heritage, whether my experience is from that of a dominant culture or a "minority" culture in a geographical location.

Even if we cannot change the experience of others, understanding these circles of experience can help me to recognize my role as dominant or targeted individuals in racial situations. Expanding my perception of culture allows me to be able to work with more diverse groups of people. This can also help to understand the role of how these cultural norms become systemic even though development may or may not have been conscious or malicious.

Other Areas of Cultural Impact and Discrimination

There are many other areas to examine the impacts of discrimination, such as sexual orientation, culture, and religion. Some of these practices can be applied to these other categories as well. These areas are not being ignored, although this text is limited to the examples of gender and race.

Cultural Awareness versus Cultural Competence

When we are limited in our perception, we can bump into things and knock things over, causing all sorts of harm, though it may be unintentional. Cultural awareness is just the beginning of seeing some of the influences of how the world around us shapes our personal beliefs, values, and emotions. As we develop awareness, knowledge, and understanding, then we can begin to move toward developing an ability to interact with individuals of other genders, races, and cultures more effectively. Developing skills to more proficiently relate to each other, we develop competence over time.

Where to Go from Here?

Cultural issues in this country will not be resolved in a few pages of a book. But perhaps this can be a starting point for individual growth and healing for some. The next steps may include:

- Self-assessment of my own limitations regarding other cultures.

- Begin to heal my own fear, anger, and hurt surrounding gender, racial, and other cultural issues.

- Continuing to increase my personal awareness of my cultural identities and the interactions with others

- Continue increasing my personal awareness of my "mental filters" and automatic "pre-judgments" of others.

- Make an effort to perceive the "lenses" of my own cultural filters, as well as those of another culture

- Continue to consider who are we, and how are we similar, behind our respective cultural "sunglasses"

- Continue to read and learn about other cultures

- Gain knowledge of other cultures

- Develop an understanding of how these "filters" impact others experiences

- Begin conversations with others who have had different experiences than you have had.

- Continue to move toward inclusiveness, neutrality, and love toward our fellow travelers.

- Continue to move toward intergenerational healing.

- Continue to move toward societal and political norms that establish system-wide fairness and equality while celebrating our differences.

- Continue to move from initial cultural awareness to a proficient cultural competency

CHAPTER 24

EMOTIONS, TOOLS FROM
AROUND THE WORLD
~~~~~ //////

*The task is...not so much to see what no
one has yet seen; but to think what nobody has yet thought,
about that which everybody sees.*
- Erwin Schrödinger

While there are many techniques and tools described throughout this book, there are a number of organized approaches used by many individuals from around the world. It is beyond the scope of this book to teach each of these methods. However, below are described some of them in case you decide to explore them further.

No one tool is right for everyone. Try different approaches to find the one, or combination of tools, that are best for you. The tools you use may change over time, as you have different needs and experiences. For example, I practiced Tai Chi for many years before discovering Yoga and eventually going on to teach Yoga and meditation practices. I am also certified in the use of clinical hypnosis. Each of these specialized tools is valuable to the right person at the right time.

Note also that each of these approaches has been subject to varying degrees of clinical research. Some may be helpful for certain conditions but not others. This review is not a recommendation of an individual approach but an overview of diverse approaches as we seek themes of effective combinations of tools.

Specialized Tools/Approaches

Yoga

Yoga is a practice that was developed 5,000 years ago. The word yoga means "to yolk," the "yolk" being a harness that goes around the ox's neck so that wherever the ox goes, the cart follows. In this way, there is union or coordination between different parts such as mind, body, or spirit.

Yoga is best known as a series of physical postures, but it also includes a comprehensive system including breathing and applications for ethical practice. The physical practices strengthen the body while helping to quiet the mind. These can be very beneficial to quiet uncomfortable moods and emotions.

In a class setting, these postures become the laboratory to practice the principles of yoga ethics. An example is the principle of doing no harm. In a yoga posture, it is important to do no harm by only practicing to the level of safety rather than pushing beyond our limits to the sensation of pain. This is an important life lesson "off the yoga mat" as well. For example, sometimes in life, we set goals that are beyond our limits, causing unnecessary pain, depression, shame, and guilt when we cannot achieve them.

There are many excellent books and videos on the practice of yoga. Many classes will be gentler or more vigorous, depending upon your physical needs and abilities. Often classes will include a range from the strengthening of the physical body, to cardiovascular strengthening and flexibility, while ending with a few moments of relaxation so that the body can integrate what it has learned.

Meditation

On the Internet, you can find many audiobooks claiming to practice meditation. Many of these may better be described as a guided meditation or visualization. These can be valuable, especially for beginners, as we learn to quiet our mind.

Traditional meditation simply involves putting my mental awareness on one thing and maintaining it there. In this way, with practice, we can increase our ability to concentrate, we reduce distracting thoughts, and move closer towards a state of contentment and happiness. While these instructions are quite simple, the practice itself includes a range of nuances. It is a way of learning about how the mind works.

One may sit in meditation for a few minutes to begin and progress up to 20 or 30 minutes, twice a day. While doing so, the mind may initially become quite distracted. This is normal. The mind will quiet down over the course of the meditation, just like a snow globe settles down when you hold it still for a few moments.

In the meantime, meditation is a practice of being aware of our thoughts and a practice of steering them, rather than being controlled by them. At first, it may seem difficult to pay attention to my breath when I have an itch. I may be tempted to be distracted by the itch or to scratch the itch fighting against this urge can make the itch even more intense. However, if I do not scratch the itch, it will go away on its own.

Further, within my meditation, I can choose to return my attention to my breath rather than watching the itch. While this is difficult to describe, once you do so, it is quite easy. It is just like changing the channel on a television set.

As you understand these principles of meditation, you can quickly see how it applies to life. Some days, I decide to watch a scary television show, and some days I watch one that makes me laugh. I am in control of this choice. Meditation helps me realize when I am choosing a certain emotion, just like choosing a certain TV channel.

Once I have this awareness, I may choose to keep it. I may find that I still enjoy going to roller coasters from time to time. However, once I understand this, I can also use it to turn my attention to the channel of emotions that is best for me at a given moment.

Mantra

A mantra can be a specialized form of meditation or a practice in itself. Mantra involves the selection of a word or phrase and repeating it over time. Like meditation, I can repeat the phrase again and again for minutes, building up to longer times.

Sometimes this can be a word or phrase in my native language, in which case it is often called an affirmation, for example:

- "I love myself."
- "I forgive myself."
- "I'm strong."
- "I can overcome this situation."

For others, it is helpful to use a mantra from another language, which can help to reduce the mental chatter. It is also believed that these sounds work directly to change the body, just as a tuning fork helps to bring an instrument into the proper key.

An example of such a mantra would be "Om Mani Padme Hum." This is one of the most common mantras used around the world. It roughly translates as an intention for a compassionate heart.

It is said that we think 90,000 thoughts a day, and about ninety percent of them are repeated. Just like exercising at the gym, the more we practice something, the stronger it gets. So, if I practice beliefs such as, "I'm not good enough," "I hate myself," or "My boss hates me," repeating them again and again all day long, would it be any surprise that I would start to feel emotions of shame and depression? In this way, actions and mantras help us to practice the repetition of positive thoughts to offset the balance of practice of negative thoughts.

It is said that if I take a spoonful of salt and put it in a teacup full of water, it will taste horrible. However, the problem is not the salt. I cannot remove the salt from life. In contrast, I can add that same spoon of salt to a five-gallon pot of water, and it is substantially diluted. I do not need to rid my mind of every salty thought, but rather I can practice tools that increase attention on the pure and sweet aspects of life to offset the fears, hurt, and griefs of life.

As we repeat our mantra, we practice and intensify that intention. It then magnifies throughout our day, shaping our mental filters, attitudes, and behaviors.

Acupuncture

Licensed acupuncturists use words, needles, and other tools intended to work on the body's energy system called meridians. These can be understood as similar to Western medicine's understanding of nerve pathways, although they are a little bit different.

These trained professionals complete an assessment and choose to activate certain points on the body where the individual is out of balance, restoring a balance between the body's systems. This approach can be used to address physical symptoms. It is commonly used for pain management, as well as emotional imbalances. Many of the examples in this book describe how emotions feed one another or interfere with one another are aligned with this system of understanding the body.

Chi Kung/Tai Chi

Chi Kung is a Chinese energy system based similar to the acupuncture system, but needles are not used. Instead, gentle flowing motions may be used to change the body system. Tai Chi is a form of this flowing motion, which also has applications as a martial art. As a martial art, Tai Chi practice listens for tensions in the body and uses them as a way to disarm the enemy. Conversely, it is a practice of listening inward to smooth any personal tensions or resistances to the flow of life. The practice suggests that as we align with the flow of nature rather than resisting it, we can experience greater health and wellness, and balance.

Yuen Method

The Yuen method is another Chinese-based approach similar to Chi Kung, but rather than the use of physical movement, it activates the physical intelligence of the central nervous system to direct the body toward health. Just as we can practice the skill of directing our breathing, this method uses innate physical intelligence to direct and strengthen other aspects of healthy functioning in the complex systems of the body.

The system also uses a series of geometric figures which magnify support to certain clusters of areas of need. Similar to acupuncture and Chi Kung, this method can be used to support both physical and emotional functioning, clearing blockages and strengthening systemic functioning of the body, bringing neutrality and balance in mind, body, and spirit.

Ayurveda

Ayurveda is a system of medicine rooted in Indian culture, about 5,000 years old. Ayurveda translates to the "Science of Life." Similar to Traditional Chinese Medicine, there is an understanding of the physical body and emotional body characteristics.

Balance is seen as the natural state of life. Imbalances are seen as fundamental to the development of symptoms and illness. These imbalances can have a range of causes such as stress, trauma, seasonal change, beliefs, and other lifestyle impacts.

Disease prevention and cure are achieved through a range of practices including diet, herbs, and similar lifestyle changes to balance the three basic energies in the body, called doshas.

Native American Healing

This tradition uses mind and body techniques to heal. Illness is seen as a spiritual imbalance that may be healed with herbs, rituals, and meditation.

Practices can also include fasting and sweat lodges to detoxify the body and prevent disease. Sweat lodges offer a communal spiritual practice for prayer and healing. In this context, the medicine man- or woman is referred to as a spiritual healer.

Clinical Hypnosis

Similar to meditation, there are many books and audios for sale that offer hypnosis for a range of conditions. These can be valuable; however, one can also seek the help of a licensed or certified hypnotherapist.

In hypnotherapy, the therapist creates a unique visualization that is personalized specifically to your needs. Since it is done in a live session, a skilled therapist can also adapt the pace and hypnotic interventions to achieve the best effects for you personally.

In general, this approach involves moving into a trance state where verbal interventions can be magnified for the greatest effect. While there are many techniques within the tradition of hypnosis, one good example is smoking cessation. The personal concern may be, "When I first wake up in the morning, I feel jittery and light a cigarette." A hypnotic intervention may involve restructuring that moment with an alternate experience. For example, "Every time I wake up in the morning, and I feel jittery, I will take three deep breaths and three slow exhalations before immediately going to brush my teeth."

Notice how this is aligned with the discussion of the brain and as well as the chapter on addiction. Specifically, it is like creating a specific detour in my neural pathways.

Law of Attraction

There has been a modern American-based movement examining the principle called the Law of Attraction. Simply put, when I put my attention on a certain feeling, it tends to magnify and expand in my life. While this may sound like a novel concept, it is easy to see how my mental filters interact with the world, creating the experiences on which I focus.

As a very simple example, my mood is what I think about all day long. If I think of sad thoughts all day, I will describe myself as sad. If I think anxious thoughts all day, people may describe me as an anxious person. If I think confident thoughts all day, people will perceive me in yet another way. My perceptions change my thoughts and my interactions with my circle of family, friends, and coworkers.

> *Watch your thoughts. They become words;*
> *Watch your words. They become actions;*
> *Watch your actions. They become habits;*
> *Watch your habits. They become character;*
> *Watch your character, for it becomes your destiny.*

-Frank Outlaw

Themes from around the World

As we review a range of tools and related treatment approaches, there are some themes that emerge.

1) Honoring the Symptom and the Whole- Across multiple disciplines, there is a general agreement that we are not "fighting" the "problem." Instead, we are listening to the lesson that the symptom teaches us, guiding us back into overall balance.

2) Understanding what lies Beneath- Across multiple disciplines, it becomes clear that often the "problem" I face is not the root of what is going on but the symptom at the tip of the iceberg. Each surface emotion interacts with my

204

entire physical system, my belief system, my memories, relationships, and other aspects of life.

3) Mind/Body/Spirit- While different disciplines emphasize one or another, there is a common theme of approaching the body system as a whole.

CHAPTER 25

POLITICS AND EMOTION
❦❦❦❦❦ ❧❧❧❧❧

Politics is a profession; a serious, complicated
and, in its true sense, a noble one.
- Dwight D. Eisenhower

We have two eyes but one vision.
- Amma

We have discussed internal emotional development, physical impacts, relationship supports, and cultural influences in concentric circles of the "whole person." We now turn briefly to the role of politics and governance, which may be one of the most difficult and serious professions.

United States, The Melting Pot

We are a country of immigrants. Grounded in respect for diversity, stronger with diversity, and a foundational principle as a "melting pot." This can create some turmoil as our personal differences arise. For example, George Washington and Abraham Lincoln were known for having differences of opinions among their Cabinets.

Our government has a history of reflecting this balance through our three branches of government, designed to maintain a balance of power. This is reflective of the themes we have been exploring, that health may lie not in the eradication of elements, but in a delicate balance of a complex melting pot.

Structures for Control of Balance

Just as we have created detailed personal practices to create a structure for ourselves, politics and government create the external structure to maintain the balance and growth of our country. When functioning well, these governmental structures stabilize and institutionalize behavior patterns that support the common good.

For example, we have a general consensus in this country that murder is not acceptable. We have laws developed to articulate this consensus as well as the consequences of violation of this norm.

Through this process, the government protects our people. Every day is possible, in part, due to the general structure of this country. I couldn't drive or have electricity to turn on the lights, without a system where these things have a balanced mechanism of freedom and protection.

Where to draw the line of the balance of freedom versus protection is largely a consensus process that develops the laws of governance. However, since we are human, sometimes our mental filters of beliefs and broad cultural experiences, though well-intended, can cause challenges.

Our Role in Governance

The work of our political leaders is to find that balance, not simply from their own view, but from the views of the people. Perspective not only begins with our personal lens of experience but must also be balanced by a broader view.

Similarly, it is the work of all of us to use our voice to educate the political process. This may be through votes, but also through a range of regular contact so that those representing us can be aware of the needs of those around them.

In order to do so effectively, it is important to educate ourselves, and to become aware of the issues that affect our lives. When communicating this awareness, it is important to be assertive, but avoid aggressiveness. We share our stories as part of a team, a community, rather than as an attempt to impose our will.

People listen better when communication is balanced and grounded in relationships.

Emotions and Politics

We have discussed different motivations ranging from fear to attraction. Motivation plays an important role in the political world, where candidates motivate individuals to vote, and constituents motivate the officials to govern in ways that protect them.

Note that this discussion is not about either political view, but about the process, as we consider where we are at in a given time, and where we would like to be.

Fear

Fear is a tool that is often used to motivate. By creating a dichotomy, or a danger that must be fought, fear rallies people to a view. It can have a strong short-term impact. For example, one may have an urgent need to "get a job" or "create" jobs. While reasonable people can disagree on things, fear can rally to a consensus.

In contrast, the use of fear as a primary motivator brings stress and undermines our basic sense of safety. By creating a "We/They" split, it can cause anger and conflict in our communities.

We are a part of the same community, just like parts of the same body. So, what happens when the right eye says to the left eye, "We don't need you anymore, your view doesn't matter or is not as important as mine"? We have two eyes but one connected vision. How do we learn to work together?

Attraction

Although it is not as urgent and flashy as fear-based approaches, attraction can be highly motivating. Hope, Greatness, Change, there are many different calls to move us forward toward success. This type of motivation tends to be more long-term and stable.

Using the job example, rather than fear driving us to "pick any job," attractive motivation calls us to consider the job market, our skills and to choose a career where we can grow and have our needs met long-term. Notice that this type of goal calls us to action and communicates the need for urgency, but without the stress of fear.

The challenge of this type of motivation is that it does not fit well onto a bumper sticker. Rather it takes some commitment to engage, educate ourselves, and understand issues deeply.

How Would We Like to Be?

Take a moment to consider how we would like to be. As we do so, this can be used as a framework to exist in a balanced and effective governance. By now, you may notice the emotional tones of these questions:

- Courage to consider opposing views
- Open to listening to all the possibilities
- Assertive vision for the future
- Personal responsibility rather than blame
- Goals-based on good policy, not politics
- Long- and short-term planning
- Partnerships for success
- Collaborations for a shared vision
- Consensus building rather than simple majorities
- Compassionate laws balancing needs with humanity
- Civility
- Respect

This collection of ideas reflect the process, not the party. These reflect progress, not perfection. Perhaps someday we will be able to more fully achieve this vision.

CHAPTER 26

NEXT STEPS

❮❮❮❮❮ ❯❯❯❯❯

You can't start the next chapter in your life
if you are still reading the last one.
- Anonymous

Where have we Been?

We have examined our internal systems of processing, coping, thinking, imagery, and emotions. Deepening our understanding, we can see some of the mechanisms that maintain these patterns, keeping us "stuck." In looking at emotions, we have considered how they interact with one another as well as specific tools for them individually. From a broader perspective, these internal experiences interact with all of our relationships, including personal, work, cultural and political views. These interactions shape and maintain our views, as well as incrementally change the experience of those around us in a complex web. As we change, our entire system changes.

It is said that we reach the finish line all together, or not at all. As I grow, I bring others along with me. Some may try to hold me back in my old patterns, but just the same, our growth helps to pull them forward as well. We are imperfect together but moving progressively closer to a world with a little more ease, understanding, and connection.

Where to go from here?

We have joined together in this journey to explore our emotions, traveled through the change process, and applied these skills in key spheres of life. Perhaps you skipped some exercises along the way. I encourage you to go back to experience them. Once we learn these new ways of being, it is time to practice.

Practice, Practice, Practice.

The Yoga Sutras of Patanjali say that mastery is developed from two key elements: practice and intensity of intention.

Practice

Just as the brain example teaches, skill grows over time through practice. How does one become an expert violinist? Practice, practice, practice. Just the same, how does one become an expert in identifying, navigating, and managing emotions? Practice, practice, practice.

This book is not a novel that you read once and are done. It is a guide with a range of tools. Choose the tools that work best for you and practice them until you fully learn their lessons and applications. Then try some others to diversify your skills.

It is said that every time we change jobs, even if we have transferrable skills, it takes about a year to fully know the job, and it takes about ten years to master it. Since most of us plan on living another ten years, why not take on the learning of mastery of navigation of my emotions? I am going to have feelings anyway, so I might as well become better at mitigating the painful emotions and maximizing the joys.

Intensity of Effort

Once you commit to practicing, you then decide on effort. I could choose to simply write one gratitude each week, or I could write ten every day. I could tell my spouse I love them once a year or twenty times a day. Whatever practices and growth areas you identify, the intensity of practice affects the speed of our progress. The more we practice and the more effort we put into our practice, the sooner we reach our goal.

Taking Stock

So, we end as we began. Remembering the questions we considered at the beginning of this book, take some time to review them again:

- Why did I pick up this book?
- What did I hope to learn?
- Was I able to learn some of these things?
- Am I more satisfied with all areas of my life than when I started?
- How would I like my life to be different?
- Have I begun to make such a change?
- Am I worthy of such a change?
- Am I firmly committed to the effort needed to achieve this goal?
- Which emotion is most troubling to me (there may be more than one)?
- Is this the same one as when we started, or is this a new awareness?
- What sensations occur in my body when I experience this feeling?

- What thoughts go through my head when I have this feeling?
- What images go through my mind when I have this feeling?
- Does it seem like this feeling is permanent?
- Is this feeling permanent?
- Am I absolutely sure?
- What does this feeling need to be able to change?
- Do I have the tools to make changes?
- Do I have a diverse toolbox of coping strategies?
- Do I know how my brain works, in basic terms?
- Do I know how my autopilot mind sets me up for trouble, or happiness?
- Has trauma affected my emotions?
- Am I aware of the emotional baggage I carry from my past?
- Am I aware of a range of causes of feelings of my experience of fear, anger, joy, compassion, respect, and love?
- Am I aware of how my emotions have impacted my relationships?
- Do I understand the role of emotional patterns in the development of addictive behavior patterns?
- Does my culture affect my experience of emotion?
- When I have made changes, do I know how to effectively make them remain consistent?

You may begin to consider how your answers have changed—perhaps deepened. This book was an introductory overview, so perhaps you learned some areas you want to continue your journey with your next book. Hopefully, you have found all that you were seeking, and more.

As We Continue...

In achieving our goals, we may find a whole new world that we had not known existed before. If I keep walking west, it may be difficult at times, but eventually, I will find this thing called an ocean. Then I will need to learn how to apply my expert walking skills to learn to swim in this new environment.

If I swim long enough, I will find a whole new country to explore, and so forth. From where I am today, I can only imagine what I will learn in the coming weeks, years, and decades. As we near the end of this book, we are really only at the beginning of an amazing journey.

Through our time together, we have looked at emotions, their process, and management, dozens of tools and approaches to understand and navigate emotions, as well as how they apply across a series of common situations. Perhaps someday these things will be taught in school, so the next generation can begin practice earlier.

Thank you for traveling with me through this piece of your journey.

I'd love to hear from you. Feel free to continue your journey with me from my website, where you will find new resources and tools at www.DrKenMartz.com

Best wishes as you continue your practice, to raise your awareness, balance your emotions, find fulfillment in life, and change the world!

RESOURCES

There are numerous resources to continue your journey.

These are just a few:

- Substance Abuse and Mental Health Services Administration (SAMHSA):
    - https://www.samhsa.gov/
- National Alliance on the Mental Illness (NAMI)
    - https://www.nami.org/Home
- National Institute on Alcohol Abuse and Alcoholism (NIAAA)
    - https://www.niaaa.nih.gov/
- American Psychological Association (APA)
    - https://www.apa.org/
- National Association of Alcohol and Drug Counselors (NAADAC)
    - https://www.naadac.org/
- National Center for Complementary and Integrative Health (Division of National Institute of Health)
    - https://www.nccih.nih.gov/health/atoz
- National Suicide Prevention Lifeline:
    - 1-800-273-TALK (8255)

ABOUT THE AUTHOR

Kenneth J. Martz, Psy.D. is a licensed psychologist working in the treatment and management of mental health and addiction for the past twenty-five years. He has specialty training in Chinese medicine, yoga, meditation, and hypnosis, as well as supervision and management.

Dr. Martz has authored over a dozen publications, including serving on eight doctoral dissertation committees. He has offered over 100 local, national, and international presentations in the mental health and addiction treatment field. You can find earlier works on Amazon in *The Downside: Problem and Pathological Gambling*, and in *A Public Health Guide to Ending the Opioid Epidemic*.

AUTHOR'S NOTE

First of all, thank you for purchasing this book, *Manage My Emotions*. I know you could have picked any number of books to read, but you picked this book, and for that, I am extremely grateful.

This is a book that started decades ago. With all the stress and isolation of COVID-19, I felt compelled to finish the work so it can be available to more people as we work together to pass through these difficult times.

I hope you were able to pause to use many of the exercises in this book, and they have helped to bring you more insight and ease in balancing your emotions. If you enjoyed this book, please take a moment to help someone else, sharing with friends by posting to social media on Facebook and Twitter.

If you enjoyed this process, I'd love to hear from you, so please take a moment to leave a review on Amazon or your preferred bookseller. Your feedback and support is needed to help improve future books and is deeply appreciated.

Feel free to continue your journey with me from my website, where you will find new resources, tools, and advance notice of new books at www.DrKenMartz.com

Meanwhile, I wish you all the best!

Free Gifts!

Be sure to check out my website at www.DrKenMartz.com for updates on free material, seminars, forthcoming books, and more.

From there, you can download a range of free tools to support your journey, such as

- **Emotion Circle**
- **How to Meditate**
- **Relaxation Techniques**
- **Manage My Emotions Checklist**

Join Dr. Ken's Meditation School, our Facebook support group with others who are beginning meditation or other life practices. You can ask questions and share success!

Other Resources

- Completing these exercises out of a book can be challenging. You can purchase an audio of many of these exercises from my training website https://drkensmeditationschool.thinkific.com

- Meditation is one of my favorite tools for emotional management. If you would like to explore meditation deeper, you may consider our Beginner's Meditation Blueprint training at my training website as well.

- For a limited time, you can access these two resources at half price by using the code **SPRINGBREAKBOOK50**

COMING SOON

Manage My Emotions *for Teens*

The Manage My Emotions journey is based on the idea that I wish I had learned these things sooner. Many readers have also echoed this concern. If you have enjoyed this material, you can soon share this with your children.

Manage My Emotions for Kids is aligned with the exercises in this text. It will help you to:

- Reinforce your learning of these concepts
- Teach your children these lessons early
- Set your children on the right track
- Open meaningful conversations and communication.

Manage My Addiction

An estimated 24 million Americans are in recovery from Substance Use Disorder. Many more experience active substance use, as well as other addictive processes such as gambling, eating, spending, and screentime.

Manage My Addiction expands on the Manage My Emotions journey with new tools and insights to guide lasting changes.

Manage My Emotions Journal

One of my most asked questions has been for support in personalizing the Manage My Emotions journey.

You can now get a copy of the Manage My Emotions Journal. The journal is aligned with the exercises in this text. It will help you to:

- Personalize your experience
- Take notes
- Track progress
- Capture insights
- Manage your mood
- Articulate your thoughts and emotions

Journaling is one of the evidence-based tools discussed in this text.

The MME Journal is available in multiple formats to fit your needs. While I prefer paper copies for my journals, you can also get your copy in eBook format. You can make notes on the page in your eBook reader, or if you prefer, the eBook version comes with a link to download and print a PDF edition.

<u>Manage My Emotions</u> *for Kids*

The Manage My Emotions journey is based on the idea that I wish I had learned these things sooner. Many readers have also echoed this concern. If you have enjoyed this material, you can share this with your children.

Manage My Emotions for Kids is aligned with the exercises in this text. It will help you to:

- Reinforce your learning of these concepts
- Teach your children these lessons early
- Set your children on the right track
- Open meaningful conversations and communication.
- Includes a downloadable Parent/Educator's Guide

Manage My Emotions:

Meditations, Visualizations, and Affirmations

The Manage My Emotions journey includes a range of meditations and visualizations. Many readers have asked to these in audio version. If you have enjoyed this material you can listen to these meditations at home.

Manage My Emotions: Meditations, Visualizations and Affirmations is aligned with the exercises in this text. It will help you to:

- Regularly practice these tools
- Easily skip to the meditation that is right for you
- Set the tone with relaxing meditative music

Purchase from Amazon or your favorite retailer.

Beginner's Meditation Blueprint

The Manage My Emotions journey includes a range of meditations and visualizations. Meditation is one of my favorite tools for success, stress reduction, and happiness.

The Beginner's Meditation Blueprint will help you to:

- Identify goals for meditation and success
- Learn the evidence base for a range of benefits for meditation
- Learn step-by-step how to begin to meditate
- Develop a plan for a regular meditation practice
- Use tools to help troubleshoot and grow your practice

If you would like to enroll in our Beginner's Meditation Blueprint training, you may do so by going to our training website https://drkensmeditationschool.thinkific.com

For a limited time, you can access these two resources at half price by using the code **SPRINGBREAKBOOK50**

Made in the USA
Las Vegas, NV
16 April 2024

88743913R00128